Easy Linux: an installation guide for adults

Alan Ward

Published by CreateSpace Independent Publishing Platform

ISBN-13: 978-1724763044

Legal Disclaimer

Although the information contained within this work is accurate to the best knowledge of the author, **no claims are made** as to its suitability for a specific purpose, nor as regards the results that may or may not be obtained by following such information.

Computer technology is a complex field of human knowledge. Technology changes over time, and what has worked for the author may cease to work later on. Additionally, each prospective user's specific hardware setup and needs are sure to vary considerably. Generic recommendations made herein consider only a typical setup and usage patterns, and may not suit a particular use-case.

In clear: the author is of the opinion that the information contained within will be of benefit to the reader. But precise results may vary. If the reader follows this guide and things come out well, this result will also be attributable to the reader's application of previous knowledge, and plain common sense. This, we consider the most probable outcome. However, if the reader takes a certain course of action based on information contained within this work and things go badly, it is on the reader and not the author. The reader recognizes that no legal recourse is available on this point.

For this reason, the author strongly recommends that the reader not go beyond his or her zone of comfort, and take all reasonable precautions before making any alterations to their computer setup. In particular, it is recommended to make suitable backups of all data that the reader wishes to retain. For a first installation of GNU/Linux, it is recommended to work only on a computer that is **not** under immediate use in a production environment.

This being said, dear reader, let us proceed...

Contents

Chapter 1

Introduction

First things first: why call this wee book "Easy Linux", and not something like "Linux for n00bs" or suchlike?

There are several reasons for this choice of title. The first is that the author happens not to like very much the rather disparaging term variously written "noob", "noobie", "n00b", etc. Every single one of is has, as some point in time, been a newbie. This is as much true in computing, as for driving a car. The best driver in the world has, at one point in time, found him- or herself in front of a steering wheel and perhaps a stick shift for the very first time – and, most possibly, been slightly intimidated by this first contact. This is OK. We got over it, haven't we? In much the same way, we will get over opening up a terminal window and typing in some commands. Yes, you can do it. Actually, you will do it, and survive the experience. And, most probably, you will look back and wonder why it took you so long to try it out in the first place.

From the above, it should be apparent that as a writer, one should not think one is addressing readers who are challenged in the intellectual department, simply because they cannot yet type in UNIX commands with gusto. Not at all. Actually, we can be sure that every single person reading this is quite good at something or other. The reader is probably a professional in his or her own domain. But, if you are reading these lines, your skill-set does not yet include GNU/Linux system management. But the fact remains that you do have skills and knowledge in your own domain, and thus are worthy of the respect of other people, be they computer technicians or not.

So, nobody will be looking down at you. No "noobing" is to be found here. This also the origin of the expression that was tacked onto the title: "for adults". It is not to say that younger readers are not encouraged, quite to the contrary. But they will not find themselves in a world of adolescents, but rather in that of ordinary, functional adults of our species. We suppose each has his or her own set of problems in mind, most of which have nothing to do with operating systems, and that the computer is seen as a tool that should function well and basically get out of our way when we have some Real Work to be done.

The beginning of this chapter may have come over as a tad trite to some, but experience does show that it is worthwhile to get things started on a solid footing. So, with that out of the way, let us get stuck into just what this book is. Over the last twenty-some years, many family members, friends and co-workers have found out that my choice of operating system is GNU/Linux. At some point in time, some of them have asked me to help them set it up on their own computers. In many cases, the operating system that was delivered on the hardware no longer gave satisfaction. In other cases, the manufacturer had deprecated the operating system, and ended support for either the hardware or the software. The user was, so to speak, on his own. This pretty much explains why I am typing this on a 2011-vintage Apple Macbook Pro which, in year 2018, cannot be upgraded to the latest Apple Mac-OS. As a result, it is running the latest Linux Mint 19 Tara (Figure 1.1)

Figure 1.1: Apple Macbook Pro (ca. 2011) running Linux Mint 19.

and doing so quite well indeed.

The interaction with friends and colleagues in this case made me notice several things. One is that most lay-people started out with a bit of apprehension when confronted with the terminal for the first time. Naturally, this does wear down as one gains some experience. Perhaps this would be a good time to give a graphical example showing how easy things can be from a user's perspective. Suppose we wished to find a file with a specific type in our Dropbox folder, for instance a LaTeXsource document. These usually have extension `.tex`. In a GNU/Linux system, we could simply fire up a ter-

Figure 1.2: Finding a file from the command line.

minal, go to the required folder, and use command find (Figure 1.2). With a little practice, this is much faster and more flexible than using a search feature included in the desktop manager. It also works on a variety of operating systems running on desktop computers, small hobbyist single-chip systems such as the Raspberry Pi, or large mainframes running UNIX.

Another fact was that they were rather dependent on me at two specific points in time. The first was to install the system in the first place, and the second to maintain their systems in good shape over the years. Actually, they were much in the same position as if they had continued to use their previous operating system, i.e. dependent on somebody with the technical know-how to perform these actions when required. Perhaps the drawback they were facing was that a certain generation of technical staff used to consider the terminal and written commands as rather difficult territory. In this, the author considers they have been misled: terminal commands are often more informative, faster to execute and suffer fewer alterations over time than most Graphic User Interfaces (GUIs).

Another point is that there used to be –at one point in time– rather less computer engineers that are knowledgeable about GNU/Linux than for some other systems that we shall not mention. This is luckily not much the case today, though the impression users get may remain. A supplementary factor is that those who are formed in GNU/Linux are often no longer in direct contact with the public, but rather quite busy setting up and maintaining servers and virtual appliances for e-commerce. The feeling I was getting was that users did wish to "go the Linux way", but were rather wary of finding themselves bereft of support should they need it. Perusing the forums on the Internet is certainly a practical means of obtaining information when necessary, but having a solid background to actually understand the initial problem and know which questions to ask is of help.

This is where this short manual comes in. Our goal will be to make the user less dependent on outside sources of information, as regards specific tasks. These have been chosen based on actual questions that Real People™have asked me over the years, and concern:

1. Setting up our base system.

2. Maintaining our software and upgrading.

3. Installing extra software.

4. Making backups of our data.

5. Firewalls and system protection.

As can be seen, these are all very basic tasks, and well within the range of operations that most users can handle with some confidence.

As to the operations that will **not** be covered in this book, we will not be speaking about the finer points of system administration, such as setting up various services or fine-tuning multiple-drive setups. These would concern, rather, a server environment and would exceed the expectations of most users of personal computers. Neither will we address programming on a GNU/Linux platform. These are both areas of interest for advanced users and technicians, and I would definitely encourage interested readers to expand their knowledge of these subjects – after covering the basics in the following pages.

A previously stated, this book has been written and produced on a computer running Linux Mint 19 Tara, typeset in LaTeXusing *TexLive*, *gedit* and *hunspell*, with graphics processing in *GIMP*, *Inkscape* and *Graphviz*. All of these software packages are easily available, and open-source. Alternatively to LaTeX, complete office suites such as *LibreOffice* usually come as standard with the operating system itself. This is a bit different from many commercial operating system, where one must start by installing the system itself, and then continue by obtaining and installing various software packages coming from different sources.

All examples in this book will be given for the Linux Mint distribution, though some major differences with other distributions will be noted when appropriate.

The Linux Mint family of GNU/Linux distributions is known for being based on Ubuntu, which in turn is based on Debian. All of these distributions share a common core of ways of performing systems operations. Other distributions based on Debian, such as MX Linux or Peppermint, also work in much the same way. Other families of GNU/Linux distributions with varying flavors in their styles of systems' administration include the RedHat distribution –and those related to RedHat such as Fedora and CentOS–, SuSE/OpenSuSE and the Arch family. The main concepts are the same, however, and much of the same software can equally be installed and used with these distributions. The actual commands vary a little, though, and the reader may be more comfortable following this manual using one of the Linux

Mint family – at least for the first time through.

Later on, gaining some experience with other flavors of GNU/Linux may be an option to consider. For example, one could be in a situation where other distributions are widely used[1].

Computer commands and addresses (Uniform Resource Locators, or URLs) on the Internet are given using mono-spaced font. For instance, the command in a terminal to list the contents of a folder would be `ls` (list directory), and the address of the author's web page is:

```
http://awardk.wordpress.com
```

Examples of commands input into the terminal will, in most cases, include both the command itself, and a sample output. The command can be recognized by its preceding '$' sign if it may be used as an ordinary user, or '#' if it must be used with administrative rights. These *prompts* are **not** input by the user. In the following example, the user has typed precisely three keys: 'l', 's', and Enter:

```
$ ls
Downloads     Images     Videos     Public
Documents     Desktop    Music
```

The subsequent two lines are the result of the command's execution, in this case a listing of the sub-folders within the user's home directory.

The prompt will be preceded, in all cases, by a text giving the user's login name, the computer's hostname, and the current directory. For instance, in: `user@user-pc:` , the user has logged in as `user`, the computer's name is

---

[1] In some scientific and business environments, RedHat and RedHat-based distributions are prolific. Using a similar –but desktop-oriented– Fedora distribution would probably be a wise move in such a situation, to gain leverage from the experience of people around the reader.

`user-pc`, and the user is currently within his or her home directory – which is what the ~ symbol means.

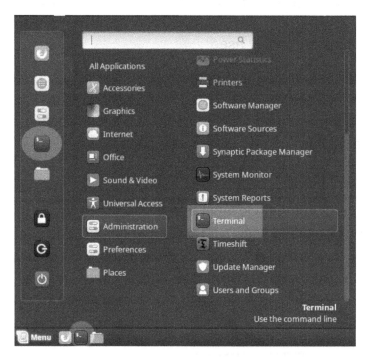

Figure 1.3: Locating the terminal, with which to input commands.

The terminal application itself can easily be found, in Linux Mint and in many other GNU/Linux distributions (Figure 1.3). There is usually a black-/white icon down in the menu bar, and also another in the preferences to the left of the main menu. If the icon is absent in these two locations, it can always be found in the Menu, Administration, Terminal.

Tip: In several places along the book, we will be inserting tips into our discourse, formatted in this fashion. They are here for a reason. Please read them carefully; they come from experience and can save much frustration in the long run.

Chapter 2

Setting up our base system

In this chapter, we will start by setting down some vocabulary that may not be familiar to the reader. However, we will limit ourselves to terms that could really matter to the average user, so aficionados may find the list of definitions a tad lacking. We prefer to call it focused, instead. This section may seem quite technical in places, but I would like to assure the reader it is necessary – if only to understand most of the literature widely available on the subject of installing and maintaining a GNU/Linux system.

Then, we will see how to choose –more or less wisely– a GNU/Linux distribution and, finally, how the installation process should go. Here, too, we will need to go into some detail about hard drives and their partitions, to decide in which place to install our new system. The end result of the chapter should be having a working GNU/Linux system all set up.

In order to follow along, it would be best to have a spare USB pen-drive you can empty and use as a boot medium for GNU/Linux. It would also be nice to have a computer with a hard drive that can be taken over completely by the new system; some pointers on this will be given along the way. The reader may wish to give the chapter an initial read-through before deciding on which of his or her computers to do the installation.

> **Tip:** This chapter sets up a lot of the groundwork for the rest of this book. However, it can also be seen as the most technical with difference. Readers who do not feel very secure with the more technical concepts of computing may read only the definitions, and skim over preparing boot media and installing the system for the time being. Having a more experienced user prepare our first GNU/Linux system for us is no disgrace[a]. At a later date, you can always come back to this chapter and do the installation yourself for your second GNU/Linux system.
>
> ──────────────────────
> [a]If you decide to follow this route, please remember to get the administrative password from whoever installed your new system. You will need it later on, to install software and for maintenance purposes.

2.1   Just what is a kernel? And a distribution?

The world of GNU/Linux and its distributions may seem a bit wild and weird to the average user of a commercial operating system. In the latter, one usually gets a complete monolithic construction, with no alternatives for each bit used in the mix. No choice can be seen as a good thing, since there is less thinking involved. In the GNU/Linux scenario, however, there is often more than one option for each bit of the operating system, so a bit more effort is needed to fit the different parts into a complete setup. To schematize, an operating system can be seen as a pile of (at least) four different layers (Figure 2.1).

At the bottom end of the pile, the **kernel** is one of the most important components of the system. This is the bit that controls access to the proces-

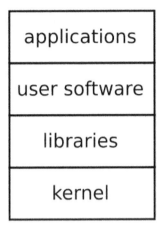

Figure 2.1: Layers in an operating system.

sor or CPU[1]. On this depends the fact that our operating system multitasks nicely without giving any process in execution the chance of running away with all available power, leaving the other processes stranded. A good illustration of this scenario that most of us will have seen at some point in time is when one ends up with a totally unresponsive computer, and no other option than a hard reboot.

The kernel is also in charge of allocating live memory or RAM[2] to each process. Needless to say, a process that somehow grabs hold of all available RAM will leave other processes starved and unable to work on any data. A good indication of when a system is low on RAM is when all processes tend

---

[1]CPU = Central Processing Unit, the chip that actually executes instructions (and costs a large proportion of the price of the computer). Examples of CPUs include the Intel Core i5, the ARM processors in mobile devices, etc.

[2]RAM = Random-Access Memory. This is where processes store data while working on them, so the size of RAM equates approximately to how many things one can work upon at once.

to slow down dramatically, and new processes cannot even start up at all.

Finally, the kernel is also entrusted with handling hardware. This is why missing *loadable kernel modules* –what would in other operating systems be called *drivers*– are almost always the culprit when a piece of hardware does not work for us. Typical examples include printers, which need modules (or drives) to translate between whatever "language" the kernel uses internally and that used by the printer. Luckily for us, nowadays GNU/Linux is quite well sorted out as regards kernel modules. Some of them come with the kernel itself, while others may be supplied by the hardware manufacturer or third parties. Most modern and widely-used hardware can usually be made to work without delving into the realm of modules. However, wireless cards and some advanced graphical cards are known to pose problems at times.

> **Tip:** When in doubt if a specific piece of hardware works with GNU/Linux, it is always best to test it. With many distributions, what is known as a "Live Image" (more on that later) can be downloaded, and used to boot a computer while making no changes to its hard drive. This is a great way to see if its WiFi card will work with our specific choice of distribution, without making alterations to the computer.
> Always bring a Live Image along when purchasing a computer. If the vendor will not allow you to boot from your image, either convince him or her to boot up the computer from their Linux distribution of choice, or go your way. Handling missing drivers/modules can be messy, obviously even more so when one lacks some experience.

Above the kernel, we find the **libraries**. Their existence comes from the realization that many programs need to perform similar actions. For instance, a web browser such as Mozilla Firefox will need to connect to the Internet,

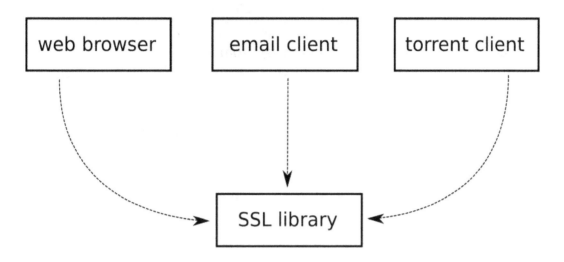

Figure 2.2: Applications invoking a common library.

probably over a secure connection[3]. But an email application such as Mozilla Thunderbird would also need to establish similar connections, and so would a torrent client such as Transmission. In all of these cases, it makes sense to separate the routines performing the secure connection from the main body of the program. These routines are placed within a so-called library, which can then be used by very many distinct user applications (Figure 2.2). There is some advantage in terms of disk space with this scheme, which had its importance in early times. However, in these days the main explanation for the widespread use of libraries is in the fact that well-tested components can be directly incorporated into a new application, without the application developer having to re-invent these routines and test them anew.

Above the libraries, all software belong to what is called the **user soft-**

---

[3]A connection such as SSL or TLS, that the user can force with the `https://` address prefix – please note the 's' indicating a secure connection.

ware[4]. This is software with which the user will interact directly. In the case of GNU/Linux, most text-based commands found in this category are directly inherited –as for their syntax and uses– from the earlier UNIX and BSD operating systems. This is a considerable advantage for technicians who need to work on computer mainframes, virtual servers and even Apple's Mac-OS: the commands are very often perfect clones of each other. Most computers with a GNU/Linux operating system will have a fairly consistent selection of such programs or commands available.

New users who are used to commercial operating systems will often be bewildered by the very many **desktop managers** available in GNU/Linux. Pieces of software such *Gnome*, KDE's *Plasma*, *XFCE*, *Pantheon* or others offer alternatives as to how the desktop is drawn on screen, how it reacts to user input, how applications are started, which menus are presented and where they are located on-screen, etc. In fact, the desktop manager chosen by each distribution becomes one of its signature features. Thus, there is not very much difference between the Ubuntu series of distributions (using Unity, and now Gnome), and Xubuntu (with XFCE) or Ubuntu Budgie (with Budgie). This variety can be a tad alarming to people who are accustomed to seeing each successive version of Microsoft's Windows (Windows XP, Vista, Seven, Eight, Ten...) come out with its specific desktop manager, which one cannot swap out for another. With GNU/Linux, although each distribution tends to favor one or other of the desktop managers, they can usually be changed at will. One could very well start out by installing Ubuntu, then install the XFCE desktop manager and Xubuntu's artwork, and end up with a very palatable Xubuntu desktop.

In a sense, desktop managers can be said to be a part of the user software layer. An installation of a specific version of KDE's plasma desktop

---

[4]Some authors would include the libraries within this class, under the name *userland* software.

manager will not be very much different from a Debian to Kubuntu distribution, or indeed under OpenSuSE or Fedora.

Finally, **applications** consist of those programs that are installed on the computer for the specific needs of each user. In this sense, they will often be tailored to his or her needs and tastes. One user will prefer to browse the web using Mozilla Firefox, while another will have only Google's Chrome browser on his system. In a similar way, there are several choices for most types of user applications, be they office suites or music players. Since the situation if very similar to other operating systems, we will not say much more about this type of software – except to note that most users will **not be allowed to install** any software at all in a GNU/Linux system.

> **Tip:** For security reasons shared with their UNIX ancestors, users of GNU/Linux operating systems require administrative privileges to make any alterations to most areas of the system. Some applications may be packaged to be installed within individual users' home directories. However, if the application cannot be obtained in this form (more on this in the next chapter), users will need the collaboration of the system administrator to install any additional software.
> So: no installing an extra web browser or a game if you do not have an administrator's password.

As a side-note, some authors prefer to refer to the operating system as "GNU/Linux". "Linux" refers only to the kernel, as well as most of the associated drivers. These are elaborated by a project initiated by Linus Torvalds, and that can be consulted at `http://kernel.org`. On the other hand, the libraries layer is constituted of numerous individual libraries, many of which are maintained by their own teams. However, some major libraries that are at the foundations of the system and a large number of basic user software pieces are maintained by the GNU project initiated by Richard Stallman (`http://www.gnu.org`). Applications are, once more, created and maintained by very many individual teams. One can see that the operating system's complete ecosystem is made up of an extremely large number of producers, though with two major players: the GNU and Linux projects.

So, at last we can explain what a **distribution** consists of. Obviously, software in each layer must be selected, and obtained from different sources, and somehow combined to work well together. In some cases, the fact that standards are in general well-respected makes such integration quite an easy task. In others, however, making all the bits and bobs collaborate with each other does give rise to problems. This is where the concept of a distribution comes in. Its task is to perform such integration. However, it does not end there. Most distributions include their own pieces of software, to facilitate system administration for end-users. A typical example is the installer, which is the application that is used to prepare the computer's hard drive and transfer the system. Another, quite important, aspect is maintaining software. As new versions of each application are made available, they must be integrated into the distribution's *repositories*, or servers on the Internet from which computers can download and install these new versions. The same can be said of Linux kernels and of libraries.

In doing so, distributions will very often check the software to make sure it complies with the distribution's own standards, before making it available to end-users. They also can make small alterations to the software, to ensure compatibility to the rest of the system.

All this should give the reader an idea of the importance of distributions and their role in making sure GNU/Linux is a viable alternative to other operating systems.

2.2   Choosing our distribution

Choosing a distribution to suit our needs is never easy. Some people tend to stick to a single distribution for long periods of time, only rarely switching to another. Other people are natural "switchers" or "distribution-hoppers", mostly when they begin to use this operating system. The best course of action for the beginner, however, is to choose a single distribution as the basis of their main work computers. Other distributions can be tested on the side, but it is best to stick to one offering at first, to gain confidence and experience. Although many of the programs and applications are the same across distributions (LibreOffice remains LibreOffice, be it upon Debian or with CentOS), details that mostly relate to system configuration can be noticeably different. This can impact your learning curve, as regards time taken to consolidate what you know.

But, how to choose a distribution?

The first aspect to be considered is what usage we will be making of our new system. There are a fair number of distributions available that have been configured out-of-the-box with specific use-cases in mind. Examples include setting up a dedicated router, converting a computer into a Network-Attached Storage (NAS) device, setting up a home movie theater, or network penetration analysis. There are dedicated distributions for each of these purposes – although it must be said that any GNU/Linux distribution can be configured to suit any of these purposes by adding the appropriate software. Even among distributions that have a more general scope, there is a clear divide between distributions more oriented towards setting up a server (CentOS, Debian, Ubuntu Server...) and those catering for the desktop market. A visit to the distribution's web page should give us a quick idea of the target audience for that specific project.

> **Tip:** The well-known web page Distrowatch (http://www.distrowatch.org) has a comprehensive list of GNU/Linux distributions (as well as some others such as BSD variants). For each distribution, links to the project's homepage are included, as well as links to third parties' reviews.

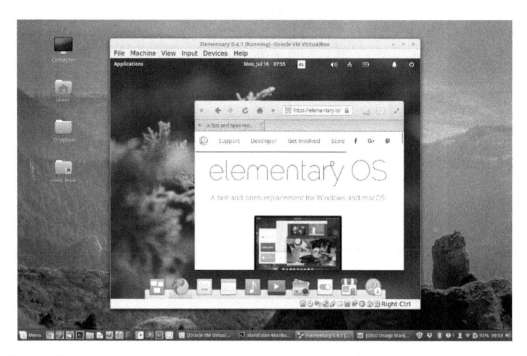

Figure 2.3: Testing the Elementary distribution inside a virtual machine on a host laptop running Linux Mint. The very same test could also be performed on a host running Microsoft Windows or Apple Mac OS, with the appropriate virtualization software (in this case: VirtualBox).

One way to test-drive a distribution that is new to us, is to install a virtual computer setup on our current operating system. Virtual computers can be created with most modern operating systems, with applications such as

VMWare[5] or Oracle's VirtualBox[6]. These virtual machines can then be configured and a different flavor of GNU/Linux installed without affecting our hard drive (Figure 2.3). This is a nice way of test-driving different distributions and seeing which suits our particular needs or tastes, before we commit ourselves to an installation.

There are, however, two main problems with virtual computers. One is that they run slowly, noticeably more so than real machines. For this reason, it can be difficult to get a sense of a particular distribution's effective responsiveness on our hardware. The other is that some distributions seem not to work in precisely the same way in a virtual environment, as opposed to physical hardware. These differences are most noticeable with heavy graphical desktops such as Gnome or Plasma.

> **Tip:** GNU/Linux, as all operating systems, is happiest when the underlying hardware is sufficient in quantity and quality. However, its needs are lesser than other operating systems. A fair bet would be a minimum of 20 GBytes of disk space, and 4 GBytes of RAM to run a modern (2018-era) distribution.
> If a Solid-State Drive (SSD) is not available, the processor is weak (think Intel Atom) or the target system has less RAM, one of the lighter desktop managers can be a good choice. Try out a distribution with LXDE, XFCE or Mate, instead of Cinnamon, Gnome or KDE's Plasma.

A second way of trying out a distribution is using that distribution's "Live Image" installation medium, if it exists. Most major distributions do have them, and in some cases it is the preferred means of obtaining and installing the system. This is in essence a compressed file-system that is distributed in the

---

[5]A commercial application.
[6]An open-source application: `http://www.virtualbox.org/`.

form of a CD or DVD image. The image is either burned into a physical CD or DVD –depending on its size– or transferred onto a USB stick. A computer can then be booted off it, and the system can be tried out **without** affecting the hard drive. The advantage of this procedure is that we can get a fair idea of the speed of execution, better in any case than using a virtual environment. If we choose to continue with a complete installation on our hard drive, we already have the boot medium set up. As for setbacks, we will need to download a complete installation medium, which in some cases can weigh in a 1.8 GBytes or more[7].

The most practical course of action would probably be to start out with a fairly well-known and well-documented distribution that is targeted at a general audience. The chances are that such a distribution will cater for most if not all needs of an average user. Linux Mint and Ubuntu on the Debian side of things, with OpenSuSE or Fedora as possible alternatives, could all be considered suitable candidates. As stated, in this book we will concentrate on Linux Mint, though this choice can mostly be seen as a case of personal preference.

2.3   Creating the boot medium and running a Live Image

The first step in installing our new system is obtaining a system image. There are a couple of considerations to observe.

- Most modern distributions offer a single type of image. This comes in an ISO file, i.e. with the `.iso` extension and internally formatted with a

---

[7]These are 2018 values; there is a tendency for boot media to continuously grow in size.

hybrid file-system. It can be burned to a physical CD or DVD: the former if the file is less than 700 MBytes in size (a rare occurrence nowadays, but can still be found for the "lighter" distributions), and the latter for file-sizes of 700 MBytes and more. It can also be written out to a USB stick, which is the more usual procedure at this time.

Some distributions offer images with two different extensions, `.iso` and `.img`. In this case, the first type can only be used in conjunction with a physical CD or DVD. The second "disk image" file can only be used on a USB stick.

- Most distributions offer a "Live Image", which can be used to test and run the system before installing it to the hard drive. However, others offer only an installable image, which can only be used to install the system on the hard drive, erasing its contents. Yet other offer both types. In this case, the live images are usually labeled as such, which pure installation images are labeled as "install" or "alternative".

- Distributions can offer both 64-bit images, and 32-bit.

  The former are labeled as "64-bit" or –more commonly– as "amd64" or "x86-64". They require a 64-bit Intel or AMD processor to run. Luckily, most computers sold since 2010 are well into this category. Moving forward, most distributions will probably concentrate on this processor architecture.

  The latter are labeled as "32-bit", "i686" or "i386". They can run both on 64-bit and 32-bit Intel and AMD processors. On newer processors, the full range of processor features will not be used, such as support for more than 4 GBytes of RAM. While not quite deprecated, this architecture should be considered to be on its way out at this point in time.

  Finally, some distributions also offer images for the ARM family of processors. These are completely different from the Intel/AMD families,

and such images will only work on specific hardware with such processors. At the time of writing, this is still a minority, with notable represen-
tatives such as the Raspberry Pi single-board mini-computers.

For the vast majority of users downloading a 64-bit ISO image is the
safest bet. For the purpose of example, I obtained this file:

`linuxmint-19-cinnamon-64bit.iso` (1.9 GBytes)

from `https://linuxmint.com/` through a straight HTTP download. Readers using the Torrent protocol may also consider this option, thus reducing
considerably the load on the projects' servers.

On most operating systems, there are options to burn a DVD from an
image. Consult your user manual for that or, more probably, take a quick
search on the Internet. However, it is clear that many users will not wish to
burn a DVD for this purpose. In fact, most modern computers completely lack
an optical drive, due to its little use.

> **Tip:** If, for whatever reason, using a USB stick to boot your
> computer is not an option for you, and your computer does not
> have an optical drive, cheap external DVD drives can be ob-
> tained that connect to the computer using USB. Such a drive
> can be used either to burn an ISO image to a DVD, or to boot
> from.

If, as will be the case for most readers, your medium of choice is a USB
stick, the drive itself should obviously be of sufficient capacity to hold the ISO
image. One should bear in mind that the drive will be completely occupied by
the image even if it has excess capacity: **any existing files on the USB will
be silently and completely destroyed!** So a quick backup of these files is
always a good move before starting.

To actually transfer the ISO file to the USB, for Windows and Mac OS users there is a modern application called Etcher (`https://etcher.io/`) that is said to work quite well and is intuitive to use.

Alternatively, the geekier solution is to use the old UNIX terminal command `dd`. This is a very powerful command that is available on UNIX computers, but also on Mac OS and any version of GNU/Linux. One would begin by plugging in the USB stick, and determining its device assignation with terminal command (actual commands may vary depending on your system):

```
$ sudo dmesg | tail
[sudo] password for alan:
[11469.049509] sd 6:0:0:0: [sdb] 3915776 512-byte
   logical blocks: (2.00 GB/1.87 GiB)
[11469.050377] sd 6:0:0:0: [sdb] Write Protect is off
[11469.050382] sd 6:0:0:0: [sdb] Mode Sense: 43 00 00
   00
[11469.051267] sd 6:0:0:0: [sdb] No Caching mode page
   found
[11469.051282] sd 6:0:0:0: [sdb] Assuming drive cache:
   write through
[11469.055437]  sdb: sdb1 sdb2
[11469.058756] sd 6:0:0:0: [sdb] Attached SCSI disk
```

In my case, the system is reporting that a new USB stick has been connected, of capacity 2.0 GBytes. This stick is now accessible as /dev/sdb.

I will unmount the drive, in case it has been automatically mounted. In my case, /dev/sdb1 (the first partition of /dev/sdb) had indeed been mounted.

```
$ sudo unmount /dev/sdb*
umount: /dev/sdb: not mounted.
umount: /dev/sdb2: not mounted.
```

Now, I can write the ISO file –currently in my Downloads folder– out to the USB stick. This is the part when any content on the stick will be completely written over:

```
$ sudo dd if=~/Downloads/linuxmint -19-cinnamon -64bit.
  iso of=/dev/sdb bs=32M
```

This operation should take some time, specially on slower USB drives. Do not try to remove the USB stick before the operation has completed. If it has a LED, wait patiently until it finally goes out.

> **Tip:** Creating a bootable USB drive using dd may be the most technical part of the installation process. It is also a step that is easy to carry out badly – and this can end up formatting the hard drive of the computer on which it is performed.
> **Exercise caution**, and consider recruiting the help of a technically savvy person to help out, if only for this step alone. If at all unsure, using Etcher is the safer option.

> **Tip:** Distributions will often offer documentation on how to burn the ISO image to a DVD or, more commonly nowadays, to transfer it to a USB image. In the case of Linux Mint, the "Create the bootable media" section of the *Linux Mint Installation Guide* (https://linuxmint-installation-guide.readthedocs.io/ en/latest/burn.html) has all the necessary information.

We can now proceed to insert our new USB drive (or DVD) in the target computer. Do so with the computer switched off. Then boot. At the beginning of the boot process, there will probably be a key that, if pressed, will allow us to choose between drives to boot from. This can be F12 (function key 12), but on some systems can also be F10 or even ESC (the Escape key). On Apple

Figure 2.4: Initial screen for the Linux Mint distribution, on booting from a USB stick.

computers, hold down the Option (Alt) key continuously. We then choose the appropriate drive –USB or CD/DVD– and hit Enter to continue. If successful, we should see the GNU/Linux distribution's initial screen appear (Figure 2.4).

Once this initial screen has come up, Linux Mint is beginning its boot process. In most cases, this live desktop will take a couple of minutes to load the kernel, the initial disk image, set the system up and finally get the desktop running (Figure 2.5). If the desktop does not come up, there may be an issue either with the pen-drive, or with the computer. Trying the pen-drive on another computer –please remember this is a **live** desktop, which will not alter the hard drive unless explicitly instructed to do so– is a way of ensuring the boot medium is good.

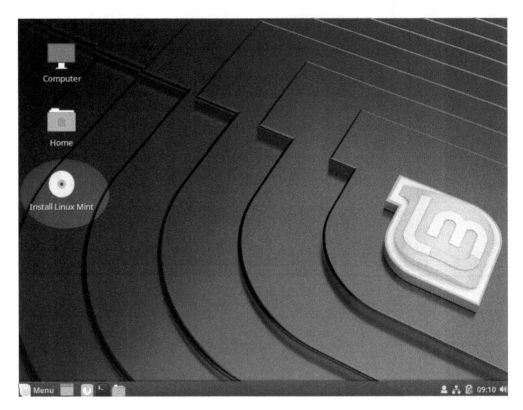

Figure 2.5: Linux Mint live desktop.

> **Tip:** If there is a major issue with the computer, it may be best to leave it and substitute on another machine. In my experience, all computers can –somehow– be persuaded to run GNU/Linux. However, there are two clear categories: the 99.99% that run the system perfectly from the get go... and the other ones. These can be trying, and require more than a little know-how to get them running.

Once our live desktop is running, it is a good time to test out most features we would like to use once the system is installed on the hard drive. Main points that deserve a little attention are:

- Does the network connection work? Can we connect to the Internet using WiFi? Otherwise, we may need to connect using a physical Ethernet cable during installation, and later install additional drivers. This is the case for most Apple products.

- Do the main applications we wish to use work, individually and together?

- Are there some things missing for our workflow? We may wish to draw up a list of software to be downloaded and installed later on.

2.4 Installing the system

At this point, we have in fact covered the most complicated part of installing a GNU/Linux system: creating the boot media and making sure our computer can boot from it. Now comes the time to commit ourselves to actually making the installation, and performing the process.

> **Tip (important!):** Installing a new operating system is always a delicate moment. There is a potential for **loss of data**. So, before going any further, it is best to make sure there is no data on the computer than cannot be wiped out without regrets.
> Also, **test** your backups to make sure that the copies of data you wish to conserve have actually been made correctly. One cannot insist enough on the importance of this action.

Tip: One way of making sure we are conserving our data is to swap out the hard drive of our computer for a fresh one. This is also a route that preserves a way to reestablish the original state of the machine: just swap the hard drive back, and we should be able to find the original operating system immediately.

This operation is usually very easy for desktop machines. As for laptops, things can be very easy indeed, for machines in which there is a specific trapdoor for the hard drive in the bottom of the computer. Alternatively, on some computer the whole bottom lid comes off using a reasonable number of screws. On the other hand, some laptop machines are not designed to be user-maintained, and in this case removing the hard drive can be rather involved. As we say, "Your Mileage May Vary".

Figure 2.6: Linux Mint: installer step 1, choosing our preferred language.

Now, once we are sure you wish to continue, let us fire up the installer – outlined in Figure 2.5– and start going. This application is divided into several steps, upon which we shall comment in sequence. The first step is our choice of language (Figure 2.6). This is fairly self-explanatory. However, it is also a good time to reflect on the many language options that are available for Linux Mint, one of its stronger points[8].

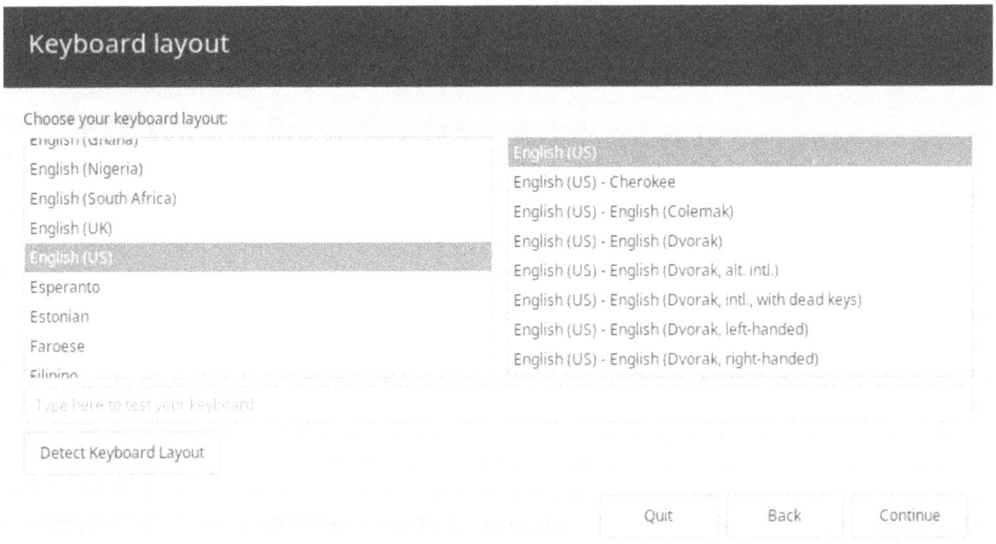

Figure 2.7: Linux Mint: installer step 2, choosing our keyboard layout.

Step 2 is also quite simple, since all we will be doing is indicating our keyboard layout (Figure 2.7). The only caveat is that many keyboards for the same language may have different physical layouts. For instance, the Spanish-language keyboards for the Iberian Peninsula and for South America have different placements for accent keys. The same applies for QWERTY

---

[8]The availability of different languages from the start is a trait that Linux Mint holds from its upstream supplier, Ubuntu. If, for whatever reason, Linux Mint does not convince us, but we need access to one of the less-common language translations, one of the *buntu distributions may be a viable alternative.

/ AZERTY / Dvorak key placement schemes. At this point, we are not yet configuring an Input Method Editor (IME) such as those used to input Chinese or Japanese non-alphabetic characters. These will be configured later on, once the system has finished installation and has been rebooted.

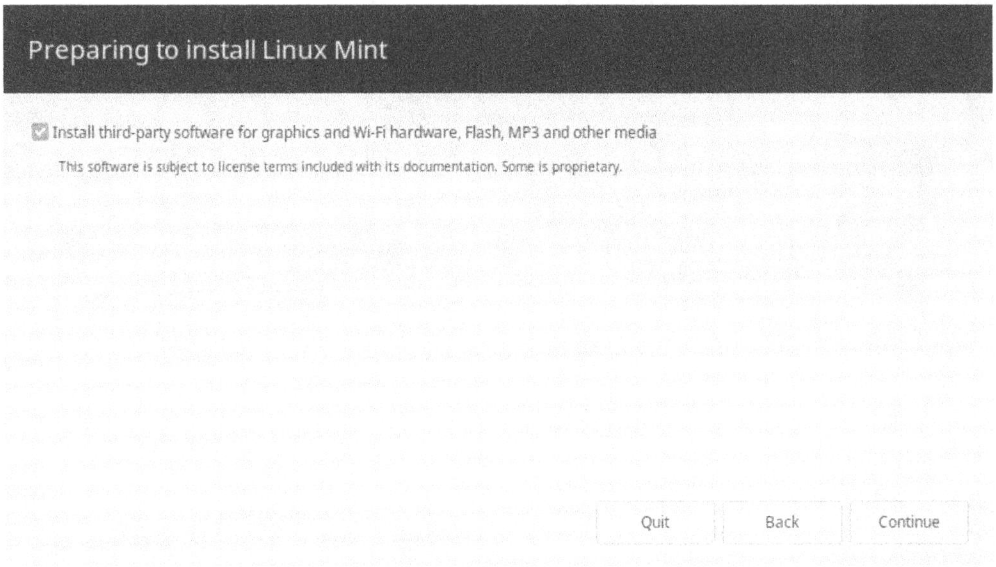

Figure 2.8: Linux Mint: installer step 3, installing extra drivers and codecs.

In step 3, we choose whether to connect to the Internet and download extra drivers (e.g. for WiFi cards) and multimedia codecs[9] during installation (Figure 2.8). This is always a good idea, though it will slow down the process slightly. Naturally, we will need to connect to the Internet to enable this. If we are not yet connected, we can do so by clicking on the network icon ⊞ or 🛜 in the lower right corner of the screen.

At step 4, we begin things in earnest. This screen may contain slightly

---

[9]Codecs are algorithms needed to read or write compressed multimedia files. Common examples are files in the MPEG-3 (`.mp3`) format for music, and the Quicktime MOV (`.mov`) and MPEG-4 (`.mp4`, `.m4v`) video container formats.

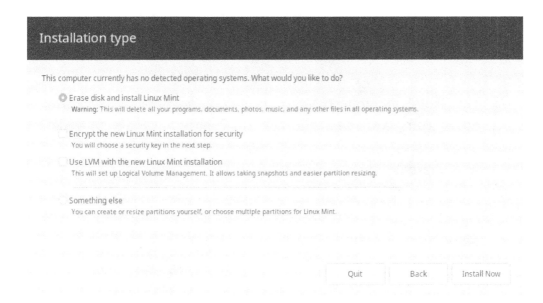

Figure 2.9: Linux Mint: installer step 4, choosing our partition scheme.

different options, depending on whether our computer has had a previous operating system, or if our hard drive is brand-new. Let us go into some detail.

A **hard drive** is a physical unit that has some capacity to store data. At the time of writing (2018), common sizes are nowadays in the 500 GByte to 4 TByte range for rotational disc drives, while Solid-State Drives (SSDs) can be anywhere from a mere 32 to about 800 GBytes. This is a domain with much movement, however, and drive sizes are rising rapidly – mostly for SSDs. These are based on computer memory chips using Flash technology, and thus contain no moving parts. This is why SSD drives are both faster in terms of data transfer, and less affected by physical movements than rotational drives. They are also lighter, and use less power to run. There is little not to like, save for their prices which are still a tad high (though dropping). Older computers will contain a rotational drive from new, though it can often be swapped out for a faster (though perhaps smaller in capacity) SSD drive.

> **Tip:** Rotational hard drives still have an advantage over SSD drives as regards capacity. For this reason, it would perhaps be advisable to use rotation drives for NAS units and large storage applications, and SSDs for desktop computers and specially laptops.

In the world of GNU/Linux, hard disk drives are designated /dev/sda, /dev/sdb, ... etc, in order of their connection to the computer's motherboard. To add complexity, optical drives also participate in this scheme, as do external drives and pen-drives connected via USB. This can end up being a little confusing for the user. The most common layout for a typical laptop being booted from a USB stick would be:

- /dev/sda: the internal hard drive.

- /dev/sdb: the internal optical (DVD) drive.

- /dev/sdc: the external USB pen-drive from which the system was booted.

If there is no internal optical drive, the USB pen-drive would be assigned the next available letter, i.e. /dev/sdb.

> **Tip:** To know which designation has been assigned to each drive in our computer, we can use GNU/Linux's `dmesg` command to access the register logged by the kernel on booting. For instance, in this setup the computer has assigned `/dev/sda` to a 64 GByte internal drive:
>
> ```
> $ dmesg | grep sda
> [    2.108788] sd 0:0:0:0: [sda] 125045424
>    512-byte logical blocks: (64.0 GB/59.6 GiB
>    )
> ```

When installing the system on the hard drive, if we choose the first available option (Linux Mint takes up the whole hard drive), the installer will set up a series of **partitions** for us. These are separate areas in the hard drive, each assigned a specific amount of space. On a hard drive with the older Master Boot Record (MBR) drive setup, the drive may be split into up to four "primary" partitions denoted `/dev/sda1` through to `/dev/sda4` (if the physical drive is `/dev/sda`. Any of these primary partitions can be further divided into "secondary" partitions, denoted from `/dev/sda5` onwards. The main difference between partition types is that early operating systems –such as Microsoft's MS-DOS– could only boot from a primary partition.

The Linux Mint 19 installer would typically create the following partitions on our drive, if using an MBR setup:

* `/dev/sda1`, formatted with file system type `ext4`[10] and used as our computer's root (main) system partition /.

---

[10] `ext4` or "extended file-system, version 4" is a type of file-system used widely under GNU/Linux. Other commonly-used file-systems are `vfat` and `ntfs` for Microsoft Windows operating systems, and `hfs` for Apple's Mac OS and iOS.

A file will be created on this unit, to be used as a **swap** space. This consists of using part of our hard drive as supplementary memory, which can save us from running out of RAM in a pinch. In previous versions of Linux Mint[11], the setup would have been slightly more complex:

- /dev/sda1, formatted with file system type ext4 and used as our computer's root (main) system partition /.

- /dev/sda2, a primary partition used as a contained for secondary partitions.

- /dev/sda5, within /dev/sda2 and used as our computer's swap space.

With the transition to computers booting using Unified Extensible Firmware Interface (UEFI) booting –including most Apple products, and Microsoft operating systems from Windows 8 onwards–, the hard drive partitioning setup has been altered. The newer GUID Partition Table (GPT) scheme now used can hold more than four primary partitions, which is why secondary partitions are no longer considered useful. On the other hand, UEFI booting requires an initial boot partition with a vfat filesystem that our computer's BIOS reads on initial boot to see which operating systems are available. Under this scheme, Linux Mint's installer will propose the following partition setup:

- /dev/sda1, formatted with file system type vfat and used as the EFI boot partition. Typically, about 192 MBytes to 1 GByte of disk space is reserved at the beginning of the hard drive for this partition, which can be accessed from the final system as /boot/efi.

- /dev/sda2, formatted with file system type ext4 and used as our computer's root (main) system partition /.

---

[11]Or versions of Ubuntu preceding 18.04.

The other options available at this stage of the installer are:

1. If a previous operating system is present on the hard drive, there will appear an option to conserve this. Space will be made for GNU/Linux by resizing at least one of the existing partitions. Obviously, at least one of the existing partitions will need to **have enough free space (12 to 20 GBytes)** in order to make a new partition for Linux. This process usually does succeed in retaining the former operating system, and the user can choose between it and GNU/Linux each time the computer is started. However, there is **no guarantee** that this will work, which is one of the reasons why making backups of our data is so important. The installation process can be quite slow indeed, as partitions are moved around and resized.

2. There is a checkbox allowing us to encrypt our disk drive (in fact: our Linux Mint partition). If used, the partition will need to be unlocked at each boot, using the passphrase entered during installation. Losing the passphrase would mean **loosing access to our system**. This option is best left to laptop computers that may be exposed to theft or that contain sensitive data.

3. These is also a checkbox allowing us to use virtual partitions (LVM). This is an advanced option most users can do well to leave aside.

Step 5 is rather more simple, consisting simply of choosing our local time zone (Figure 2.10). On GNU/Linux (and UNIX) computers, the computer's internal clock is general set to Universal Time (UT); knowing the time zone allows the system to present time and date in the correct locale.

In step 6, the installer requires us to create our default user (Figure 2.11. This first user can be seen as a normal user, with no special privileges.

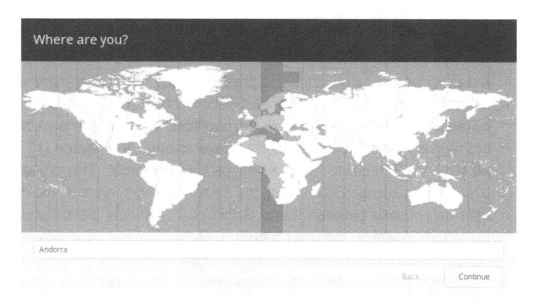

Figure 2.10: Linux Mint: installer step 5, choosing our time zone.

However, being inside a special group of administrative users, he or she can obtain administrative privileges when needed. Other users can be created later, once our system is up and running. In most cases, these other users will only have normal user permissions.

The distinction is quite important in GNU/Linux, since only users with administrative permissions may alter the system configuration and installed software. In general terms, normal users can each affect only their own personal home folder.

As to the options available, having our user log in automatically can be useful when the computer is to be used only by the default user. The screen requiring entering a password is bypassed, and the default user's desktop is immediately displayed.

On the other hand, this setup may also be seen as a security defect.

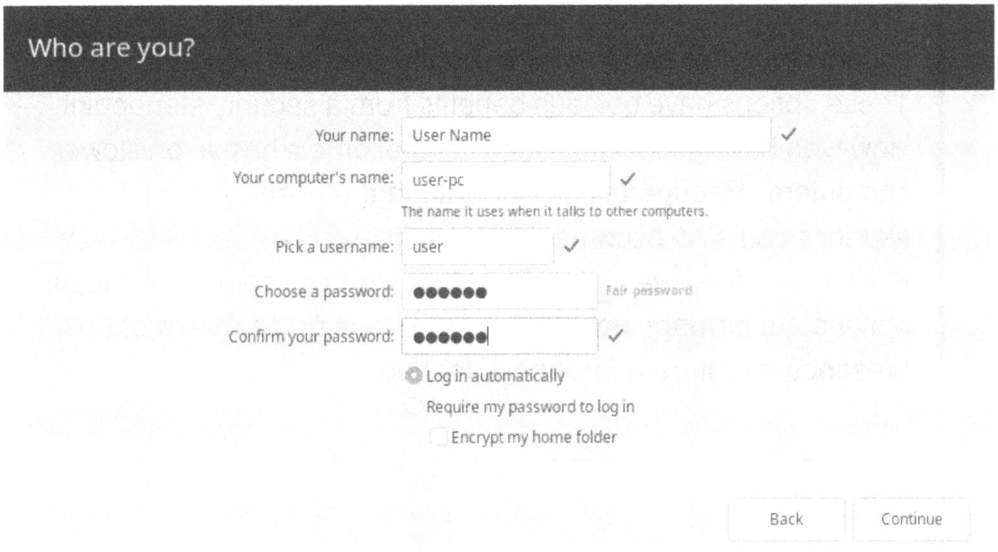

Figure 2.11: Linux Mint: installer step 6, creating our default user.

People working in an environment where computers are shared between many users may prefer to have each user enter his or her password: when this option is checked, the option for automatic login is naturally grayed out.

Encrypting the main user's home directory is an option that now exists for the Linux Mint distribution, but has been removed from Ubuntu's offering. With this option, the user's directory is encrypted with a passphrase only he or she knows. In contrast to whole disk encryption, encrypting the home directory will allow the computer's main user to keep his or her data in an encrypted form, while allowing other users to access and use the computer. Whole disk encryption would require the computer's owner to give the disk decryption passphrase to all users.

Tip: Encrypting either a user directory or the whole disk does impact computer performance slightly, and also usage of RAM. These options have obvious benefits from a security standpoint. However, having them activated can become a hassle on slower computers. Recuperating user data in the event of a total system loss can also become problematic.

For the first time we install GNU/Linux on our computer, these options are perhaps best left aside. However, be aware of their presence for future reference if needed.

Figure 2.12: Linux Mint: installer step 7, rebooting our system.

After completing step 6, one should see the installer chug away at installing various software packages, and then configuring our new system. Depending on our hardware and if we have requested the installer to pull in drivers and updated versions of software from the Internet, the process can take as little as 4 minutes (measured on an Intel Core i7 and internal SSD drive, not connected to the Internet) or as much as an hour (on an Intel Atom and internal rotational drive, downloading fresh software from the Internet). After the process is complete, the final step (Figure 2.12) is to reboot our system. During this process, a message should appear asking us to remove our boot media (DVD or pen-drive), and to confirm it by hitting the Enter key.

Chapter 3

Maintaining our software, and upgrading

Once we have a GNU/Linux system newly set up, the fun can begin. In this chapter, we will start by getting to know our new system. Then we will perform some fine-tuning to get things exactly as we wish, both as regards hardware and drivers, connecting to networks, and the software aspect of the system.

As usual, a nice place to start is, in computer parlance, RTFM: "Read The Fine Manual". In our case, Linux Mint helps us out, since a welcome screen is presented on boot (Figure 3.1). This screen can be dismissed –for good– if not required, but it could be helpful at the very least to have a quick look at the section on Documentation the first time we see this `mintwelcome` application.

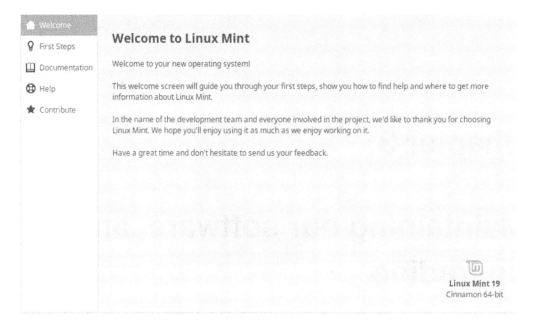

Figure 3.1: Linux Mint: the welcome screen after rebooting our new system.

3.1   Updating our system

Although our system has just been installed, this does not mean that it is completely up to date. To understand this point, let us take a look at the production cycle along which a typical distribution is prepared:

1. Software packages are pulled from the various original software projects. These are usually obtained in the form of source code, i.e. applications written in a high-level programming language such as C, that need to be compiled or turned into executable formats.

2. The distributor makes sure these applications are compatible with other applications and the distribution's base system. They are then compiled, using the same compiler and base library versions as the rest of

the distribution.

3. The software packages –already compiled and ready to be installed on a computer– are made available to end users on the distribution's servers. This is called a **software repository** for that distribution.

4. An installer disk image –often in the form of a live image– is prepared and made available to download in the form of a `.iso` or `.img` file.

The last stage of this process is quite lengthy in terms of computation. So, some distributions perform this stage very often, perhaps once a day, in what is called a **rolling release** model. Most distributions, however, do not. Instead, the **main release** images are created once, in stage 4. A user who installs this initial version has a computer with the versions of software that were current at the date on which that release was published. However, newer versions of software packages may have been published at a later time. These can then be pulled down and installed, effectively updating the user's system without having to download and re-install a complete installer disk image.

As a side-note, from time to time distributions that go a long time between main releases can make available what are designated **point releases**. These are not much different from the main releases, except for containing software that has already been updated. So a user who downloads and installs one of these point releases will need to update only the software that has been made available since the date of publication of this point release, instead of going all the way back to the corresponding main release.

> **Tip:** Although Ubuntu and Linux Mint major versions are released on a bi-yearly schedule, this does not mean that when a new major version comes out, one should immediately rush to obtain and install the new version. Quite on the contrary, some administrators consider it wise to **wait for the first point release** to appear before upgrading, when the inevitable initial issues have been ironed out.
>
> Linux Mint also benefits from the five-year support period granted to most Ubuntu LTS versions. In practical terms, this would mean that one can run Linux Mint version 18 up to the end of year 2021 and still receive software updates during this period. Linux Mint 19 –which appeared in 2018– should probably receive support up until the end of 2023.
>
> This gives users ample time to reflect on the pertinence, or not, of upgrading their computers to future versions 20 or 21 during this time period. Most professional users tend to dedicate one computer for the purpose of testing new versions, reviewing that all is well before committing production machines to the new operating system. This is true for any system, and may often be imitated by users running more than one computer in their homes. The take-away would be **not to upgrade** all your computers to a new version **at once**.

At the time of writing, Linux Mint version 19 –named "Tara"– has just been made public, on June 29, 2018. This is the initial (main) release of LM 19. As for the previous Linux Mint 18:

- The initial release of LM 18, code-named "Sarah", was made public on June 30, 2016.

- Point release LM 18.1, named "Serena", was published on December

16, 2016.

- Point release LM 18.2, named "Sonya", was published on July 2, 2017.

- The final point release for version 18, LM 18.3, was named "Sylia" and published on November 27, 2017.

There is no fixed schedule for publishing dates for Linux Mint. However, recent versions have been based on Ubuntu's Long-Term Support (LTS) releases. These com out each two years, as in Ubuntu 14.04 released in April 2014, Ubuntu 16.04 in April 2016, Ubuntu 18.04 in April 2018. Linux Mint 19 is based on Ubuntu 18.04, so will probably be current through to 2020, with point updates coming out possibly every six months[1].

On the practical side of things, the first thing to do with our new operating system is to upgrade the information on software packages in the repositories, and then upgrade packages as necessary. There are several ways of doing this, both using text-based commands in the terminal and graphical user interfaces. However, experience shows that graphical interfaces tend to be slow, inefficient, and have to tendency to change from version to version. For this reason, in this book we will concentrate on text-based commands, in line with our target audience.

Let us start by opening up a terminal, from the Menu, Administration or directly from its black/white icon in the lower panel of the desktop. Begin by gaining administrative privileges:

```
$ sudo bash
[sudo] password for alan:
#
```

---

[1]There is no written contract to set a given timetable in place. While many distributions like to maintain a specific rythm, specific events may make it adviseable to lengthen or shorten the period between major or point releases.

Obviously, you will be greeted initially as your own user login, instead of `alan`, and the name of your computer will be whatever you called it during installation. For instance, at this time I am seeing a prompt formed by `alan@alan-MacBookPro: $`, where `alan` is my user name, and `alan-MacBookPro` is my laptop's host name. There are two further important bits in this prompt:

- `~`, which tells us where we are located in the folder tree on our hard drive. In this case, we are inside our home directory. `~` is shorthand for `/home/alan` (my user's home directory).

- The `$` sign at the end of the initial prompt tells us that, on opening the terminal, we were working as a normal user without administrative privileges. After authentication using our own password, the prompt now ends with the `#` sign. This confirms we are now acting as user `root`, or administrator of our system.

> **Tip:** A feature that has been known to surprise new users is the fact that passwords do **not appear** on screen, as they are typed. Do not be put off by this, the terminal is taking into account each character that you type! Simply continue typing, and end with the Enter key at the end of your password.
> This feature has several reasons for being, one of which is to avoid the potential for a third party to snoop and read your password from behind your back as you type. This may be useful not only in a workplace environment, but also when invoking administrative privileges in a cafeteria or other public place.

Let us begin by retrieving the lists of updated software packages available on the repository servers:

```
# apt update
```

```
... [many lines of text]
269 packages can be upgraded. Run 'apt list --
    upgradable' to see them.
```

This means that 269 among the software packages already installed on our new system have seen more recent versions appear and be published in the distribution's repositories. Since this example is for the initial (main) release of Linux Mint 19, it is not surprising that a large amount of packages have been upgraded since the release publication date. Let us now upgrade them all on our system:

```
# apt upgrade
... [many lines of text]
269 upgraded, 0 newly installed, 0 to remove and 0 not
    upgraded.
Need to 231 MB of archives.
After this operation, 7634 kB of additional disk space
    will be used.
Do you want to continue? [Y/n]
```

Let us go over this. The first line reproduced here –which is conveniently towards the end of the output, and thus stays on screen– gives us a summary of the actions to be performed. The 269 packages that need to be upgraded will be so. No new packages will be added to our system. No old (obsolescent) software packages will be removed. Finally, no packages that would need an upgrade have been left aside for whatever reason.

The system will need to download a total of 231 MBytes. This is a fair amount, giving us the idea that some rather large packages will need to be updated. This is often the case for web browsers such as Firefox (50 to 60 MBytes), or office suites such as LibreOffice (in excess of 200 MBytes). On the other hand, smaller packages can weight in a as little as 1 to 2 MBytes.

After installing so large a volume of updates, one would expect the hard drive to fill up quite a lot. This is not the case here, since we are replacing older versions of these software packages with new ones. This is why total hard drive occupation will only go up by about 8 MBytes.

Finally, the `apt` command requests permission to perform the update. Acceptable responses would be 'y', 'Y' or 'yes' to agree, or 'n', 'N' or 'no' to abandon. The capital 'Y' in the query indicates this is the default choice, so we can also agree by simply hitting the Enter key.

We should then see the system commence by downloading a series of packages, and continue with a series of actions that include "Installing", "Setting up"", "Processing", etc. Once these have been completed, our system has been upgraded to the current state of all software available.

> **Tip:** Although the new packages replace the older ones and, thus, little extra disk space is taken up, one must bear in mind that the actual software archives have been downloaded. They are still stored in a cache on our hard drive, and do tend to take up some space –231 MBytes in this case–, which can be reclaimed by cleaning up the cache:
>
> ```
> # apt clean
> ```

If we are curious as to how much space is taken up by our new system, we can invoke the `df` command, and search for the line ending in /:

```
# df -h
...
/dev/sda1   12G    5.9G    5.3G    53%    /
...
```

In this example, we are using the first partition of our hard drive (`/dev/sda`), which has a –rather small– total capacity of 12 GBytes. 5.9 GBytes or 53% of this has been used at the time being. This compares rather nicely with other (commercial) operating systems, that often run up into the 20 to 30 GByte range, even before web browsers and office suites are added into the software mix.

3.2 Installing extra drivers

If, previously to installing the system, we were able of running our hardware without issue, the chances are that we will require no supplementary drivers. The Linux kernel has a large amount of various drivers, organized into categories. A look in the appropriate system folder (for kernel modules) can convince us of this fact:

```
$ ls /lib/modules/*/kernel/drivers/
acpi        dca        hv         mailbox    nvdimm
ata         dma        hwmon      mcb        nvme
atm         edac       hwtracing  md         parport
...
```

However, as commented, some specific drivers may be lacking. The major areas which can be problematic are WiFi cards, and audio or video specific devices. In this book, we will concentrate on WiFi, under the supposition that a larger demographic will find itself with this problem.

Up to this point, we have already been in situations where a connection to the Internet is needed, for example to upgrade our system. This can be performed perfectly well using a physical cable (Ethernet) connection. However, for regular use of the computer, it may come in handy to set up the WiFi card that most modern computers have installed.

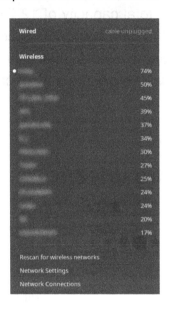

Figure 3.2: Selecting a WiFi connection with the Network Manager.

If the Wifi card has been correctly detected and activated, simply click on the Network Manager or , and select your desired network using its SSID, in the usual manner (Figure 3.2). However, if we do not see a list of base stations in the Manager, we will need to investigate further.

There are several tools available to troubleshoot network connections. The first, present in almost all GNU/Linux distributions, is `ifconfig`. This command allows us to see the details of any <u>active</u> network connections as regards their IP addresses:

```
$ ifconfig
enp2s0f0: flags=4099<UP,BROADCAST,MULTICAST>   mtu 1500
        ether 40:6c:8f:14:8e:06   txqueuelen 1000   (
           Ethernet)
   [...]
```

```
lo: flags=73<UP,LOOPBACK,RUNNING>  mtu 65536
        inet 127.0.0.1  netmask 255.0.0.0
        inet6 ::1  prefixlen 128  scopeid 0x10<host>
  [...]
wlp3s0: flags=4163<UP,BROADCAST,RUNNING,MULTICAST>
  mtu 1500
        inet 192.168.0.104  netmask 255.255.255.0
          broadcast 192.168.0.255
        inet6 fe80::cdeb:dbd6:6721:6da5  prefixlen 64
          scopeid 0x20<link>
```

Here, we have a first interface, enp2s0f0, using an Ethernet physical cable. Most Ethernet interfaces are readily recognizable by their device identification starting with letter 'e', though the actual code used depends on the physical hardware and varies from computer to computer[2]. However, this connection is not active, and for this reason we have no IP address on this interface. The most common reason would be that the cable has not actually been plugged in.

The second network interface, lo, is the local interface. This interface is always there, is always called lo, and always has IP address 127.0.0.1 associated to it. It is mainly used for IP-style communications *within* our operating system, and needs to be present for the system to work correctly. However, by its very nature it is actually useless to connect to other computers and to the Internet.

The third and last interface, wlp3s0, is a Wireless interface. And yes,

---

[2]Previous versions of GNU/Linux named Ethernet interfaces eth0, eth1, ..., and wireless interfaces wlan0, wlan1, ... This has been deprecated, and modern Linux kernels use the representation shown here. The actual code used will depend on which physical card is used, how it is connected to the motherboard, and in which position (slot). Luckily, users do not really need to worry about this.

it can be recognized by its initial letter 'w'. This interface is active and connected, and has received IP address 192.168.0.104 from the WiFi access point or router. Obviously, the details on the reader's computer may vary, but this is the type of result we are looking for.

If the computer has **not** been connected correctly to the WiFi access point, even if the wireless card has been identified, the wireless interface may not appear in the list given by the ifconfig command. To ensure our card has been detected, even if the connection is not active, we can use the low-level command iwconfig:

```
$ iwconfig
lo          no wireless extensions.

enp2s0f0  no wireless extensions.

wlp3s0    IEEE 802.11   ESSID:"xxxx"
          Mode:Managed   Frequency:2.417 GHz
          Access Point: EC:08:6B:6F:B5:EA
          Retry short limit:7   RTS thr:off
          Fragment thr:off
          Power Management:on
```

This command can tell us about any wireless cards present in our computer, which access point (SSID) they are connected to, and even on which channel or frequency.

Now, it may seem that a wireless card that has been detected correctly by the operating system should work "out-of-the-box". Unfortunately, this is not the case. The device drivers for wireless cards tend to need a specific fragment of code –the so-called "microcode"– in order to work correctly. However, manufacturers of wireless cards have a varied track record as to communicating the necessary codes. Some, such as Intel, do tend to publish their codes freely. For this reason, it has been easy for the developers of the Linux kernel to incorporate the necessary codes into the kernel to make use of their products. Unfortunately, other manufacturers have not been so forthcoming. There has been a tendency towards secrecy, perhaps so as not to compromise potential industrial advantages over their competition. In any case, their microcodes have not always been released in a timely manner, if at all. The only official support given to users is often in the form of executable drivers for one of the Microsoft operating systems.

This leaves the user at the mercy either of programmers writing code allowing using Windows drivers under GNU/Linux –with varying results, depending on the quality of the original manufacturer's code–, or of others who analyze the actual hardware, perform a reverse engineering, and come up with an open-source drivers. These often work quite well, but have not been officially sanctioned by the hardware manufacturer. In such cases, many distributions of GNU/Linux tend to balk at including the drivers because of potential issues related to intellectual property management.

Linux Mint is one of the distributions that take a more pragmatic approach to the question. There does not seem to exist a tendency, in real life, for hardware manufacturers to sue software developers who program drivers for their devices. Naturally, this may change at some point in the future. Meanwhile, however, Mint does provide a route for computer users seeking to actually set up their devices and use them in the intended manner. In the case of WiFi drivers, the easiest option to seek and install whatever drivers are necessary is to use the graphical installer found in the Menu, Administration, Driver manager. Since this application can make alterations to the system configuration, initial authentication is required. If you are using the default user with administrative permissions, simply introduce your password here (Figure 3.3):

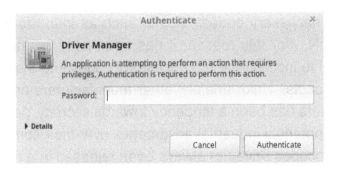

Figure 3.3: Unlocking the Driver manager.

Once running, the Driver manager will take some time to refresh data from the repositories on the Internet. An active network connection will be needed, so do not disconnect your physical cable for the time being.

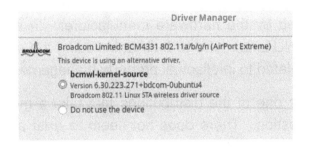

Figure 3.4: Using the Driver manager to configure a WiFi card.

In my case (Figure 3.4), a Broadcom WiFi card has been detected. Though re-branded by Apple as the "Airport Extreme", what is important is the actual chipset. The infamous BCM 43xx series has been widely used, not only by Apple but by many WiFi card manufacturers. The Linux STA driver has now been activated, and we should now be able to configure the wireless network in the usual way from the Network Manager in the lower right corner of our screen (or).

> **Tip:** If no WiFi networks are detected after installing new drivers, it may be necessary to reboot the Network Manager or –perhaps easier for the average user– to simply reboot the whole computer. When the system comes back up, WiFi networks should now be seen.

3.3 Language support

As in the Ubuntu distribution and its derivatives, language support is quite good in Linux Mint. However, language support does depend on a series of software packages being installed on our system. Packages for a specific language are often indicated with a special code, such as `de` for German, `el` for Greek, etc. In some cases, variants may be indicated using a double code, such as `zh` for Chinese, but `zh-hans` for the use of simplified characters and `zh-hant` for traditional characters.

Each application developer may decided to include any language packages either within the main software package for their application, or as separate packages. For large projects, the latter solution is preferred, leading to the presence in the repositories of a number of translation (or "locale") optional software packages. Examples include:

- `language-pack-gnome-ca` for the Catalan translations for the Gnome desktop (and Cinnamon).

- `language-pack-kde-it` for the Italian translations for KDE's plasma desktop.

- `firefox-locale-ga` for the Gaeling (Irish) translations for Mozilla's Firefox.

- `libreoffice-l10n-te` for the Telugu translations for the Libreoffice suite.

- etc...

Another aspect includes the use of an Input Method Editor (IME) in order to introduce specific character sets, mostly when the language in question uses one or several non-alphabetic writing systems. The most often used system in modern GNU/Linux distributions is either `ibus` or `fcitx`, with perhaps a tendency favoring the former for languages of the Indian Subcontinent, and the latter for East-Asian languages such as Chinese, Korean, Japanese and others. Each language can be configured with one or several input methods. For instance, for the Chinese language, packages include the following:

- ibus-pinyin

- ibus-table-jyutping

- ibus-table-stroke5

- ibus-table-erbi

- ibus-table-wubi

- etc...

It is relatively easy to install each software package separately, as we shall see in the following chapter. However, to manage simply all these aspects of language support, a specific application has been included in Linux Mint. Go to the Menu [Menu], Preferences, and Languages, or choose the Languages icon from the Control Center (Figure 3.5).

Here, in the first place we can configure the language used as default for this specific user's interface. Different users can choose different languages,

Figure 3.5: The Languages application.

which explains why this initial screen is available to all without needing to authenticate as administrator. In the same way, each user can specify which units to use for dates, monetary units, and so forth. This allows the combination seen in the Figure, where the English language (with American spelling) is specified for the user interface, but the Euro will be used by default for money.

> **Tip:** In Figure 3.5, one can see that character encoding is UTF-8. This 8-bit version of Unicode is standard on GNU/Linux systems, as well as other modern operating systems. It is perhaps best to retain this encoding, although some rarities may appear when exchanging files with other computers where a different encoding is used; specifically when non-standard characters are used within file names.
>
> With modern file formats, very few encoding problems, if any, are encountered within the actual contents of files.

The third button in the Language application allows the system admin-

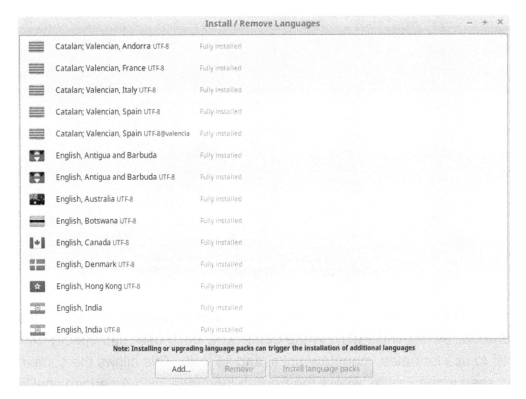

Figure 3.6: Installing or removing language packages.

istrator to specify a given combination as standard across the system. New users of this computer will begin with this configuration, though they may alter it for themselves at will.

Finally, the fourth and last button allows the system administrator to enter his or her password, and install or remove language packages (Figure 3.6).

> **Tip:** If the computer was not connected to the Internet during installation, non-English language packs may not have been downloaded and installed at that time. It is best to use the Languages application to review the status of individual languages. In Figure 3.6, all language packages are up to date and their status is indicated in green. Yellow or red information strings are presented when packages are not up to date or have not been installed.

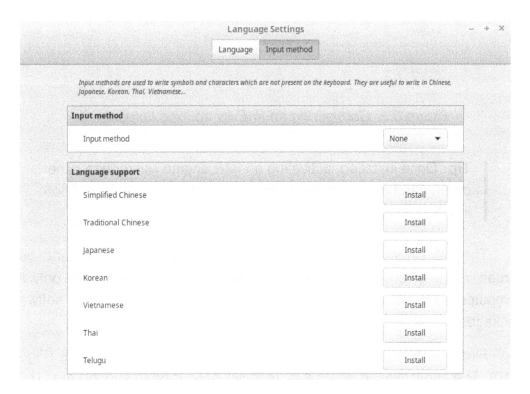

Figure 3.7: Installing IME support.

Back to the main screen of the Languages application, there is a separate tab available to configure the IME (Figure 3.7).

This provides a simple, one-button way of installing full support for introducing each specific language, including the IME engine in itself and fonts that allow the correct reproduction of the language character set[3]. For instance, choosing "Traditional Chinese" will require introducing your password anew, and install both the `ibus` and `fcitx` packages with their optional packages for traditional characters, as well as the well-known Uming font. One should then choose one of the IME engines in the "Input method" box (Figure 3.8).

Figure 3.8: Configuring an IME for specific languages.

> **Tip:** Once installed, activating an IME engine will require either closing and restarting the user session, or –preferably– rebooting the computer.

The IME engine will show an icon down in the lower right corner of your screen. Initially, an IME such as `fcitx` will be configured to use only the computer keyboard. Additional engines –already installed from their software packages– must be added to the list (Figure 3.9).

Finally, the IME may be used to input different character sets (Figure 3.10). The application in which it is used will only need to support the UTF-8 and UTF-16 encoding styles; this means that just about any native GNU/Linux window should handle inputting localized characters with no drama. Even a

---

[3]Unfortunately, not all languages are catered for. Other language packages must be configured manually.

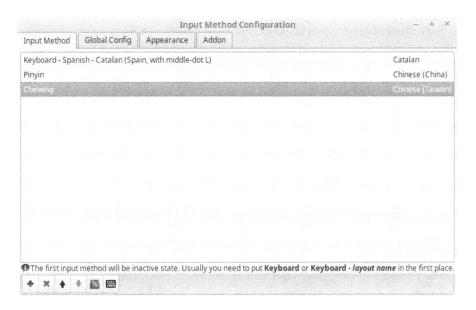

Figure 3.9: Configuring *fcitx* with various engines.

lowly terminal is well capable of doing so. Switching from one input engine to another may be done either by using the configuration button in the lower right panel, or with the Control+Space key combination, rotating between different input engines.

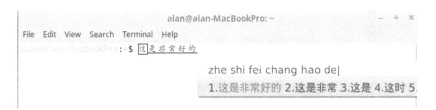

Figure 3.10: Using an IME.

3.4   Other bits and bobs

One particular feature that does tend to get a bit on my nerves is the desktop's tendency to block the screen after some time (Figure 3.11). Though it can be seen as an important security aspect if one tends to leave one's computer unlocked in an environment where prying eyes lurk, this feature can become a hassle when working at home or in a somewhat more controlled environment.

Figure 3.11: Locked out of our screen.

Figure 3.12: The screensaver control panel.

There is an option to easily configure the behavior, either leaving the screen completely unlocked, or setting a longer timer. Go to the Menu, Preferences, System settings, and choose Screensaver (Figure 3.12). The "Settings" tab contains the appropriate controls.

3.5   Maintenance in the long run

Maintaining a GNU/Linux system actually takes very little effort. Perhaps the most important part is keeping the software up to date. This can be done from the terminal. Periodically –once a week or once a fortnight– run the sequence of commands to update software package lists and upgrade any new packages, as discussed:

```
$ sudo bash
# apt update
# apt upgrade
```

There are several graphical applications that purport to perform the same actions. For instance, Linux Mint comes as installed with the Update Manager, whose icon can be seen in the bottom lower panel when this service is active: . This piece of software works as advertised, and may be helpful to users more used to running graphical software. However, in my view –and that of many professional systems administrators– the text-based `apt` command is far superior in that it gives the user a clearer feedback on what is happening "under the hood", so to speak.

> **Tip:** Maintaining our software up-to-date is nice. But the inherent stability of GNU/Linux means that software –with a support cycle of up to five years– can sometimes outlast the physical components of our computer. A failing hard drive is a very real danger to contend with on this time-scale, and more so on maptop computers that are used on the move.
>
> The only real solution to this kind of failure is to have backups of our data, and to keep them up-to-date. More on this in a later chapter.

Finally, even though we just installed our new system, it is always nice to think already about its replacement. There is no real reason why computers cannot keep running passing the five-year mark, specially if one does not need the latest and greatest to keep being productive. In that case, we shall need to upgrade our version of GNU/Linux[4]. In the case of Linux Mint, upgrading our system would concern passing from one major release to another; i.e. going from LM 18 to LM 19, or –in year 2020– going from LM 19 to LM 20 when it comes out. Upgrading a minor release, e.g. from LM 19 to LM 19.1 or LM 19.2, is not considered a major upgrade and will, in fact, be almost transparent to most users.

With Ubuntu and Linux Mint, upgrading is an operation that can be undertaken in two different ways. In the first place, the **Update Manager** application can inform us of the appearing of a new version. We can then use the same graphical software to download the appropriate software packages, and upgrade our entire system. This route has the advantage of conserving user date, as well as our selection of applications – some of which may have been

---

[4]This is even more the case for distributions that focus on cutting-edge software, as opposed to Linux Mint's more conservative attitude. To take an example, in the Fedora series each version tends to receive support for only eighteen months – after which, upgrading is definitely in order.

added to the system and are not present on the Live image. On the negative side, numerous software packages must be downloaded, and this operation must be performed for each of our computers. Even individuals tend to have more than one computer nowadays, not to speak of businesses. So, upgrading our system may become a tedious process depending on the speed of our connection to the Internet and the number of computers involved.

> **Tip:** If we are set to upgrade more than one computer, consider doing so *one at a time*. After the first computer has been completed, verify everything, and more so if upgrading to a very recent version. Linux Mint does not usually break things, but since major versions are based on major LTS versions of Ubuntu, at times the upstream provider does introduce alterations in the system. This has been noticeable during the upgrade from LM 18 (based on Ubuntu 16.04) to LM 19 (based on Ubuntu 18.04).

The second method for upgrading our system is to simply install the new version **on top** of the existing one. This "nuke-and-pave" approach simply consists of creating our boot media for the upgraded version of the Live image, booting from that and following the same process as for an initial installation. If doing so, in the step concerning partitioning and disk usage the installer will give us an option to replace the previous version with the new one (see Figure 2.9). Be warned, however, that **the contents of our hard drive will be erased**, both the system and user data.

There is an option that has been used successfully to conserve user data, which is to choose option "Something else". In this, we could manually choose the partitions on which to install the new version of the operating system. We can then choose **not** to format these partitions, thus conserving user data and much of the system configuration. However, this does require some confidence in oneself before attempting it, specially if we need to make sure user data is conserved.

This second route is perhaps best tried out for the first time on a computer (or several computers) for which we are not concerned as regards conserving user data. Only with some practice should it be attempted on our daily work computer.

> **Tip:** When performing a system upgrade:
>
> 1. Make sure we have a copy of all user data on another computer or support. Also, make sure it is current!
>
> 2. Choose the Update Manager route if at all unsure of our own capabilities.
>
> 3. Choose the nuke-and-pave route if we really need a fresh, clean system with a lot of our "old stuff" cleaned out.
>
> 4. Did I mention making a backup of our data? If in doubt, make a second copy, on another physical support[a].
>
> ---
> [a]Please forgive the insistence, but all of us have got burned at some point by formatting an existing system **without** previously making sure we had sufficient backup copies of files we wished to keep.

Chapter 4

Installing extra software

In this chapter, we will examine the different options to search for, find and install software on our system. The Live images supplied can often offer enough applications for common tasks such as browsing the Internet or editing texts. However, GNU/Linux is all about choice, and there exist alternatives for each task that each user is free to examine and perhaps adopt, if they suit best their own workflow. Supplementary software may also be a necessity.

4.1   Installing from the repositories

The concept of a software repository has previously been hinted upon, when we referred to updating our new system. At that time, using the `apt` command we downloaded and updated the various software packages in our system. Some packages will have retained their original versions, as present on the Live image. Other packages will have been upgraded to newer versions, made available by the distribution at a date between when our Live image was published and when we decided to install it on our system.

The very same `apt` command may be used to search for and install new pieces of software.

> **Tip:** The `apt` command is, in fact, only one piece of a complete ensemble that work together inside the *Advanced Package Tool* infrastructure. Original developed in conjunction with the Debian distribution, this system is now at the base of most software package management for Debian, Ubuntu, Linux Mint and their derivatives. Other commands include the more basic `apt-get`, the `aptitude` full text-based management environment, and several other tools.

Figure 4.1: Standard graphics applications available in the Linux Mint menu.

A simple example will suffice to show the potential of this system. The Live image for Linux Mint contains several tools to create and manipulate graphics, including *Simple scan* and GiMP, the *GNU Image Manipulation Program* (Figure 4.1). However, the existing applications do not seem to include a photo manager application. A simple web search online could give us several possible candidates, such as *darktable*. However, is this application directly available from the Mint repositories?

To find it, begin by opening a terminal window and gaining administrative rights. You will need them, not for performing searches but in order to actually install any new software:

```
$ sudo bash
[sudo] password for user:
#
```

It is always good practice to begin by renewing the package lists, so let us initiate this session with a quick update. even if it has been a mere few days since our last system upgrade, there may very well have been some changes in the available packages. If there are any upgrades to be done, let us perform them.

```
# apt update
Hit http://archive.ubuntu.com/ubuntu bionic InRelease
  [...]
Fetched 1982 kB in 2s (981 kB/s)


Current status: 34 (+34) upgradable, 270 (+67) new.

# apt upgrade
  [...]


34 upgraded, 0 newly installed, 0 to remove
and 0 not upgraded.
```

At this point, all available upgrades –all 34 of them– have been installed. Now, let us search for *darktable* within the repositories:

```
# apt search darktable
p   darktable - virtual lighttable and darkroom for
 photographers
```

Software package darktable is indeed present in the repositories, as noted by the initial 'p'. It is not yet installed, which would have been indicated

by an initial 'i'. Let us find our more about this package before installing it:
[breaklines=true]

```
# aptitude show darktable
Package: darktable
Version: 2.4.2-1
State: not installed
  [...]
Uncompressed Size: 16.3 M
  [...]
Homepage: http://www.darktable.org/
  [...]
Description: virtual lighttable and darkroom for
 photographers

 Darktable manages your digital negatives in a
 database and  lets you view them  through a zoomable
 lighttable. it also  enables you to develop raw
 images and enhance them.
  [...]
The core operates completely on floating point
 values, so darktable can not only be used for
 photography but also for scientifically acquired
 images or output of renderers (high dynamic range).
```

We now have quite a complete idea about what darktable is and can do for us. We also know about the project and its web page, and can consult it for more information if needed. Finally, we know how much space will be needed to install this application on our system: in this case, 16.3 MBytes (although the compressed file will be smaller during download).

Also of interest is the version number of the program, as it stands in the

Linux Mint or Ubuntu repositories. At the time of writing, we were offered version 2.4.2, in a packaging format altered by the Ubuntu project and noted with the tailing -1. However, the Darktable project was already at version 2.4.4, which shows how it may take a little time (from several days to a couple of months) for an application's latest version to appear in a distribution's repositories. This may be for the best, since it gives each successive version of the software a little more time to mature before being release on unsuspecting users.

If we decide this application is right for us and wish to go ahead and install it, we can simply:

```
# apt install darktable
```

During the installation process, the application's various files –executable programs and libraries– are each installed in their various directories, and a new icon appears in the desktop menu's list of graphical applications (Figure 4.2):

Figure 4.2: Darktable is now present in the Linux Mint menu.

In this example, we started by identifying a photo manager on the web, before search it in the repositories. Applications can also be found directly within the repositories, specially when their names are indicative of the function. For instance:

```
# apt search photoalbum
```

```
p    kphotoalbum - tool for indexing, searching and
     viewing images by keywords for KDE
```

As indicated by the initial 'k' in its name, the kphotoalbum application is based on the KDE technology. It has more or less the same functionality as darktable, though with a different interface. There is absolutely no difficulty in installing both applications side-by-side:

```
# apt install kphotoalbum
```

and then trying both applications out (Figure 4.3).

Figure 4.3: Both Darktable and KPhotoAlbum, together in the Linux Mint menu.

The user will often find at least two different applications that perform the same tasks, much in the same way a Windows' user may opt for the *Microsfot Edge* web browser, or *Mozilla Firefox*, *Google Chrome*, etc. In the case of GNU/Linux, there is a tendency to offer one application based on the Gnome desktop technology and the GTK widget set, and another application based on the KDE desktop technology and the Qt widget set. The KDE application can usually be identified by the presence of the letter 'k' within its name.

Tip: Choosing between applications of Gnome or of KDE lineage is mostly a question of taste. Although Gtk-based applications tend to integrate better into the Gnome desktop and Linux Mint's Cinnamon, and Qt applications integrate into KDE's Plasma desktop, many users will choose based on personal preferences and on an application-by-application base. For instance, a Linux Mint Cinnamon user could very well prefer the *Amarok* music library manager (based on Qt) to *Rhythmbox* (based on Gtk). This mostly a question of personal taste.

Tip: Each application will need a series of libraries to be present on the user's system, which it depends on to render graphics, play music or other tasks. When installing a Qt-based application in a Gtk-based system —such as Linux Mint— for the first time, the required Qt libraries will not be there. However, apt knows about these **dependencies**, and will pull down and install whatever is necessary. This is why installing kphotoalbum in Linux Mint will end up in a 91.1 MByte download, which may be seen as rather large for a simple photo management application. Most of these "extra" bytes are the Qt libraries themselves. Subsequent installations of other Qt-based applications will not need to download these libraries once more.
It must be stressed that dependency resolution is rather automatic in the APT system.

To finish up on the APT series of commands, there are several graphical applications that purport to give us access to the same functionality. One of them is *Synaptic*. This cross-distribution software manager allows us to refresh our package list from the repositories automatically. We can then peruse software packages by state –installed or available but uninstalled–, by type of application ("Section"), or filtering using other criteria (Figure 4.4).

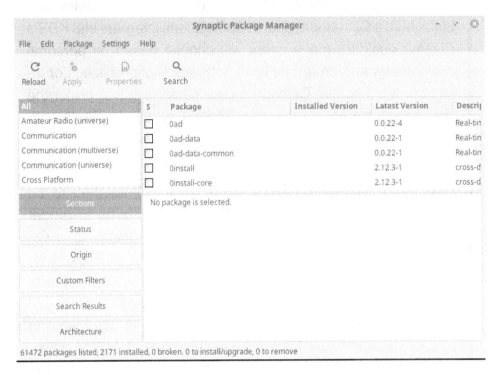

Figure 4.4: The Synaptic package manager.

If not yet installed, Synaptic can be made available in the terminal by:

```
$ sudo apt install synaptic
```

4.2   Direct package installation

The teams behind some applications choose not to make their source code available. For this reason, they would be best classified as *freeware* instead of proper *open source software.* As a consequence, the team behind GNU/Linux distributions can neither access their source code, nor tweak them to fit in with the rest of their software. These applications will, in general, not be available in Ubuntu or Linux Mint's repositories[1].

The people behind these decisions will surely have their own reasons for this stance. Perhaps they prefer to keep a firm hold on their intellectual property, which may be understandable when it is, in fact, a business that does the development. Perhaps their business model requires them to have a grasp on the number of end users who use their products. The world of web browser is, perhaps a great example to illustrate this point:

- *Mozilla Firefox* is made available mostly in the form of an executable program. This is what most end-users will be interested in, after all. But the source code for the program can be readily downloaded and examined, if one so wishes. It can be found on the web at:

```
https://developer.mozilla.org/en-US/docs/Mozilla/
    Developer_guide/Source_Code/
    Downloading_Source_Archives
```

- *Google's Chrome* operates on a dual basis. The flagship version of this browser is made available to end users only in executable form, for a number of operating systems. However, this non-open version is accompanied by a truly open-source version of the browser, *Chromium.* Chrome cannot be installed from Linux Mint's repositories. On the other hand, Chromium is freely available using `apt`:

---

[1]One notable exception to this general tendency concerns firmware for processors or device drivers, which can be found in the repositories, but only in binary (compiled, or executable) form. It would seem that this exception is made mostly for expediency, since these "blobs" of binary code are often needed in order to use the hardware at all.

```
$ sudo apt install chromium-browser
```

- The well-known *Opera* browser also follows a freeware model, not open-source.

In any case, we are not here to judge neither the developers of these applications, nor users who decide to use them instead of other, more open, alternatives. Users wish to do so can download versions for GNU/Linux of the two freeware browsers, at `https://www.google.com/chrome/` for Google's Chrome and `https://www.opera.com/` for Opera.

For applications such as these, there may be two different file styles available. One uses the `.rpm` extension, and is suitable for distributions of the RedHat family. Besides RedHat itself, these include CentOS and Fedora. The other –which concerns us here– comes with the `.deb` extension. These packages are built for Debian (from which the extension comes), Ubuntu distributions and Linux Mint.

Let us suppose we have downloaded these packages, and have them on our desktop (Figure 4.5). Now, remains the question of how to install them:

Figure 4.5: .deb files for Chrome and Opera, on our desktop.

One option would be to simply double-click on the package. This should launch the graphical installer `gdebi` automatically and, after authenticating ourselves with our password, perform the installation for us (Figure 4.6). After the installation has completed, we can close the gdebi application window:

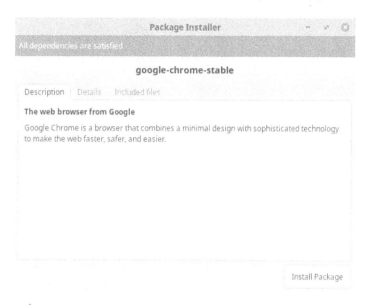

Figure 4.6: Installing a .deb file graphically with gdebi.

This procedure is very simple to use, and will suit most users perfectly. However, it perhaps does not give all required information when things go wrong. This is a rare case, but can happen nonetheless. An alternative means of performing the installation is, as usual, using terminal commands. We shall:

1. Open a terminal, and gain administrative rights using sudo.

2. Navigate to the desktop, or other folder in which the files we previously downloaded are stored.

3. Install the files using the dpkg command[2].

---

[2]Obviously, please substitute the correct file name.

```
$ sudo bash
[sudo] password for user:
# cd Desktop
# dpkg -i opera-stable_54.0.0.2952.64_amd64.deb
```

> **Tip:** Most GNU/Linux distributions have *autocompletion* acti-
> vated. This feature allows us to complete item automatically,
> when our meaning is clear to the terminal from the context. En-
> tering long, and complex, file names is a case to point. In the
> previous command sequence, one could perform the final com-
> mand by typing:
>
> ```
> dpkg -i opera
> ```
>
> and then hit the Tabulation (TAB) key. If there is only a single
> possibility to complete this file name, the complete name will
> be unfolded in place, and all we need to do to complete the
> command is hit the final Enter key.

Once the new web browsers have been installed, by either process,
they should immediately become available from the Menu, alongside existing
applications (Figure 4.7):

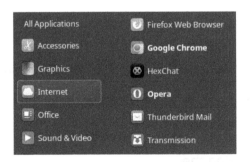

Figure 4.7: Three different web browsers, installed on our system.

> **Tip:** Many applications installed from a .deb file will add them-
> selves to our APT package source list. This means they will be
> upgraded alongside with other software packages, as needed,
> whenever the `apt update ; apt upgrade` command sequence
> is given.

4.3   Containerized software packages

Until this point, we have been working within the APT software package system. The main aim of this technology, at the time in which it was developed,
was to enable a software developer to unite in a single package a series of
files that then need to be installed into various directories. For instance, a
typical piece of software may need to:

- Install its main executable file (which will be directly invoked by the user)
  inside folder */usr/bin*. This is where most user-oriented programs are
  stored, in binary (executable) format on many UNIX and GNU/Linux
  operating systems.

- Create a new subfolder in */usr/lib* to store are additional libraries it may
  require during operation.

- Create another subfolder in */usr/share* to store artwork, icons, or other
  graphical items.

- Make en entry inside */etc*, the folder used for system configuration.

This spreading out of files all over the computer's file-systems can raise
questions about maintenance, and even about security. It is also not always
convenient for the end user, since they will need access to administrative

rights in order to install any new software. This is no big deal for a computer used only by its owner –such as a typical laptop– but can become a hindrance in large organizations.

On the other hand, users of Apple's Mac OS are long accustomed to applications being available in the form of a single file, that is simply deposited on the user's desktop, and may be directly executed from there. No installation is required to system areas on the computer's hard drive, and thus no administrative rights are required to install the application. Applications can also be transferred from one computer to another through a simple copy-paste operation[3]. What most OS users perhaps do not realize is that these application files are, in reality, a complete file-system in compressed form – but that does not show its .zip extension.

In recent years, this concept has come to the GNU/Linux ecosystem, with a twist. To enhance security, most **containerized software** will be able to run only within its own file space. This is done to minimize the possibility of applications interfering with each other, or with the main operating system. At this time, however, there are several such systems available. Some, but not all, focus on being usable on many various GNU/Linux distributions.

> **Tip:** Containerized software relies on each application holding its own copy of the libraries used within the application itself. Thus, on a typical system, various containerized applications could very well have replicated copies of a same library. As the reader can imagine, this is not very efficient from the standpoint of disk space.

---

[3]It must be noted that such is not the case for applications that, under Apple's Mac OS, require administrative rights. These still need to be installed in the traditional manner.

> **Tip:** Typical use-cases for containerized software would include testing a brand new version of a particular software alongside an existing version. This would allow us to test the newer version and ensure it integrates well into our workflow, before committing to a complete installation.
>
> Another typical use-case would be when, for whatever reason, we need access to the very latest version of an application, and this has not yet been made available within our distribution's repositories.

4.3.1 Snaps

One example of such containerized system are *snaps*, developed by Canonical, the company giving support to the Ubuntu distribution. Originally targeted at a now-defunct mobile version of the distribution, this technology has been adopted with some eagerness by proponents of cloud technologies and the Internet of Things (IoT). In Linux Mint 19, the snap server *snapd* is not installed by default, so we will need to begin by installing it using the APT mechanism:

```
$ sudo bash
[sudo] password for user:
# apt install snapd
```

For instance, we can install the Inkscape vector graphics editor[4] using a snap. The syntax for the `snap` command is quite similar to that of `apt`. In a terminal, let us begin by search for Inkscape within the available snaps:

```
$ snap search inkscape
```

---

[4]Inkscape may be seen as a more lightweight alternative for Adobe's Illustrator. The project's homepage is at: `https://inkscape.org/en/`.

```
Name        Version   Publisher   Notes   Summary
inkscape    0.92.3    inkscape    -       Vector Graphics
    Editor
```

This is actually the very latest version available at the time of writing. We can compare it with the version available from the distribution's repositories:

```
$ apt show inkscape | grep Version

Version: 0.92.3-1
```

We can see that in the case of Inkscape, the repositories' version is also up-to-date. In such a scenario, our recommendation would be to install the version in the repositories through APT, since downloading the extra bytes of a snap would give us no appreciable advantage. However, for illustrative purposes, we will perform the installation as a snap. As when installing packages with APT, administrative privileges are required since the resulting application will be installed to a system folder, and made available to all users of our computer:

```
$ sudo bash
# snap install inkscape
2018-08-03T10:09:09+02:00 INFO Waiting for restart...
inkscape 0.92.3 from 'inkscape' installed
```

The user may notice that the download seemed larger than usual. This is a true impression. Furthermore, the first time we use the snap mechanism, the system will need to download and install some extra components such as "snap-core", which also slows things down a bit.

However, at the end of the process, the new Inkscape application is available, and integrated into our system menu (Figure 4.8):

Figure 4.8: The Inkscape snap, inside our menu's section for graphical tools.

> **Tip:** The new snap application may **not become visible immediately** within the menu. In such a case, simply log out, and then log back in again.

4.3.2 Flatpak

The flatpak infrastructure follows a similar pattern to snapd. The base application –flatpak itself– does need to have been installed previously on our system. Linux Mint users are lucky, since this has already been done for them and Flatpak is installed by default starting from Linux Mint version 19. For previous versions, and for Ubuntu distributions, follow the instructions available on:

    https://flatpak.org/setup/Ubuntu/

Once Flatpak is working on our system, let us download and install a typical application many users of other operating systems will be used to having, such as Spotify. Begin, in a web browser, by navigating to one of the main repositories for flatpaks, FlatHub. Its web portal is at:

    https://flathub.org/home

Now, find the application we wish to install, and click on it. The specific application page should come up, and now we simply need to click on the "Install" button (Figure 4.9):

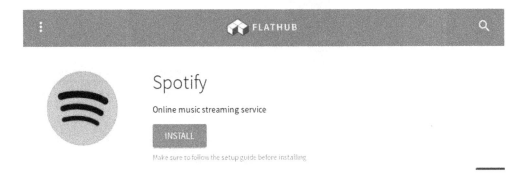

Figure 4.9: Installing a Flatpak from our browser.

Now, our web browser in itself does not know what to do with the short descriptive file that is downloaded from FlatHub. It now needs to pass this information on, for example to one of the possible graphical software managers, appropriately named *Software Manager* (Figure 4.10):

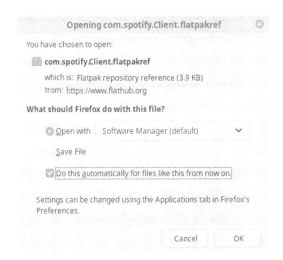

Figure 4.10: Continuing to install a Flatpak is Software Manager.

When this –rather lenthly– process is finalized, one should have the new application freshly installed on or system (Figure 4.11):

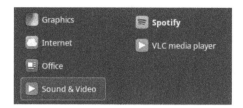

Figure 4.11: Our newly installed Spotify flatpak application.

4.3.3 AppImage

Contrary to the *snap* and *Flatpak* mechanisms, *AppImage* is more user-centered. Applications in this format tend to be graphical, and are installed by the user simply downloading it to their desktop and executing it from there.

> **Tip:** AppImage files tend to be more easily installed by the end user. No supplementary software (snapd or flatpak) is needed.

Also contrary to the previous two systems, AppImage does not seem to work within the centralized repository paradigm. This means we will need to navigate to each different project's homepage to determine if that particular application is, or not, available in AppImage format. This has some drawbacks, such as the loss of the convenience given by a centralized system. On the other hand, many previous users of Microsoft Windows are perhaps best accustomed to this scheme.

> **Tip:** Since we will be downloading AppImage files from various places, it pays to make sure we are downloading **from a well-known source**. In the same way that users of other operating systems have gotten burnt by download software of sketchy origin, malware is very easily hidden within an AppImage. So make sure you get it from a safe source.

To take an example, let us install one of the two best-known video editors for GNU/Linux, *KDEnlive*. Though designed for KDE's Plasma desktop, it will work well with other desktop managers, such as Linux Mint. Begin by using a web browser to navigate to the project's home page:

```
https://kdenlive.org/en/
```

Now, navigate to the Downloads page, where one will find a section on "Cross distribution packages". Right enough, this application is available in AppImage format, as well as many others (Figure 4.12):

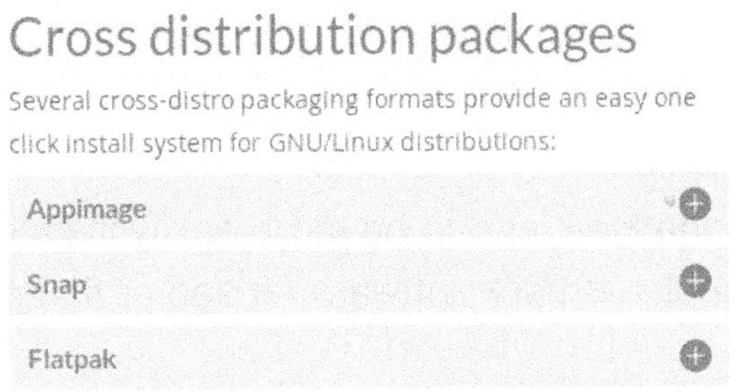

Cross distribution packages

Several cross-distro packaging formats provide an easy one click install system for GNU/Linux distributions:

Appimage ⊕

Snap ⊕

Flatpak ⊕

Figure 4.12: The KDEnlive application is available in several forms, among them AppImage.

Go ahead and download the AppImage file. As with Apple's Mac OS .dmg files, this is simply a compressed folder that simply needs to be downloaded, and not opened with any specific program (Figure 4.13):

If using the default configuration for Mozilla Firefox or most other web browsers, the downloaded file will be stored in the Downloads folder. Using the file icon on the desktop, navigate to this folder and drag KDEnlive over on to the desktop. Now, we need to make the AppImage file executable. Right-click on the file, and select *Properties*. Now choose the Permissions tab, and allow executing as a program (Figure 4.14):

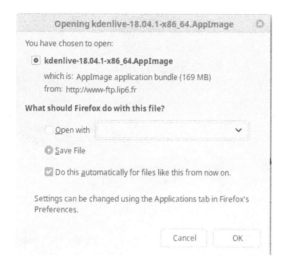

Figure 4.13: Downloading the AppImage file.

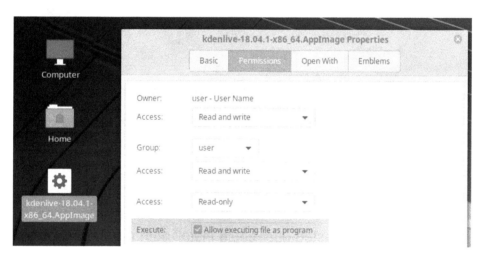

Figure 4.14: Making the AppImage file executable.

That is all: our new application is installed and can be used directly (Figure 4.15):

As a side-note, we can observe that, at the time of writing, KDEnlive was

Figure 4.15: Executing KDEnlive from an AppImage file.

available in version 18.04.1 as an AppImage. This application is also present in the distribution's repositories. However, it was still at version 17.12.3[5]. The differences between versions may, or may not be of importance to each individual user. The interested user could install both the AppImage and the version from the repositories (using the `apt` command) on their computer for comparison.

```
$ apt show kdenlive | grep Version
```

---

[5]KDEnlive's version 17.12 was made public in December of year 2017, while 18.04 initially came out in April of 2018.

```
Version: 4:17.12.3-0ubuntu1
```

4.3.4   Compiling software from source

Once upon a time, users of a GNU/Linux operating system often needed to compile software from source. This process meant having the compiler software installed on one's computer, obtaining the source code, eventually modifying it to suit one's actual distribution setup, and finally compiling the source code into executable form.

Luckily for end-users, this option is now very much superseded in actual practice, since most applications destined for non-technical users are available in several executable formats. The only exceptions the author can think of where an end-user would need to compile software would be for:

- Very old applications, that are no longer supported, and for which no suitable modern equivalent has been found. These are very rare, but do exist (think specific file formats).

- Applications that were developed for other platforms, such as versions of UNIX or BSD. These are often found in scientific and engineering environments.

The best advice in such cases, specifically for newer users, would be to seek guidance from more experienced technicians. A background in compiling or integrating systems written in the C or Fortran programming languages may be helpful, according to the nature of the original code. However, it can be stressed that running source code originally written for mainframes or high-end workstations decades ago on a modern GNU/Linux personal computer can be a viable option.

Tip: Even though most users will never compile their own programs from source code, they should be aware that if the source
code is made available, this possibility does exist. They should
also recognize the fact that if someone –whoever it is– can
examine the original source code, this constitutes an informal
guarantee against the inclusion of malware inside the application, and in favor of eliminating any bugs present in a timely
manner.

This is the essence of open-source software, indeed.

Chapter 5

Making backups of our data

Once we have our new Linux Mint system all set up, with the applications we wish to use, it is time to think about the data we will be creating, and how to make sure it can be kept securely and retrieved at will. Now is, in fact, the best moment to think about this, since it may affect how and where we store our files on the hard drive.

5.1   So, what is a backup, and what is it good for?

The main idea behind a backup is, simply put, to have a second copy of our data. To elaborate on this concept, we can distinguish between:

- *Local* backups, versus *remote*. Local backups are performed on the computer itself, which then holds two copies of the same data. Obviously, this technique is next to useless against most causes for data loss, such as a bad hard drive. It is used mainly when we need to perform some operations on the data which would alter it. Having a copy of the data is a simple means of being able to go back to the data's original state, if our alterations are not successful and need to be reversed. To take a simple example, editing a copy of a text document instead of the original would be an example of the use of a local backup.

Remote backups, on the other hand, are performed on some other physical support. One could make a copy of the data on a second computer, on an external drive, or even on a web service in the so-called "Cloud" (e.g. Google Drive, Dropbox, etc.). They are considered more secure against the loss of data due to physical hazards, such as a bad hard drive, or even against human error – such as overwriting a file that we did not mean to. Naturally, having a remote backup that is geographically at a certain distance from our main computer is an extra safeguard. For instance, one could have a backup stored at a friend's house, in a different locality. This technique has several drawbacks, but may be useful in the case of data that does need to be conserved, but may not need to be accessed very often. The family collection of photographs comes to mind.

- *Complete* backups, versus *incremental*. A complete backup means precisely what the term suggests: all data elements are replicated. The backup holds a complete copy of the original data set. If the original copy is lost, any data may be directly recovered from the backup.

An extended version of this technique would be to make a copy not only of the data, but also of the operating system. In essence, one is "mirroring" the complete computer with another machine. This technique is often used with servers, in situations where losing a machine would mean losing service for users, potentially also incurring economic losses due to lost opportunity. When one server goes down, a secondary server is waiting to take over while the main node is being repaired and put back on line. Performance may be degraded, but users will always receive some level of service. The technique may be replicated even on an individual basis, for example holding a complete copy of all of our important data on two different laptops.

However, making a complete backup copy can take some time, specially when user data contains large items such as video files or music. In an incremental backup, data items are analyzed for changes. Only items that have been altered since the last backup took place are copied over, thus reducing the time and bandwidth necessary to perform the backup and transfer data. This technique does have its own drawbacks, such as needing some processor power to perform the initial analysis. The initial backup copy will also take some time, since at the beginning of the process the backup copy is still blank, and all data items need to be copied over.

- *Archived* backups contain a copy of all data, but –due to using compression or other space-saving techniques– each individual item of data may not be accessed directly. This is a liability if, for some reason, we need to recover a single file or piece of data.

> **Tip:** A well-balanced scheme of backups will combine several techniques, gaining the benefits of each in turn. The trick to this is working along different schedules: immediate copies, versus middle-term backups, and then a longer-term archival strategy.

To propose an example system that is easily implemented by an individual user, it may be beneficial to:

1. Keep documents on which we are constantly working in two copies: one locally on our hard drive, and the other in the "cloud", using a service

such as Dropbox (automatic synchronization) or Google Drive (manual). These files would be stored, for instance, in the `/home/user/Dropbox` folder. Synchronization should take place, ideally, every time a file is modified, or at the very least at the end of a work session.

2. Make remote copies of all documents being added or modified, on a monthly basis. If we have a free computer available to us, making this a mirror image of our main computer and synchronizing files once a month is a great way of making sure we are never left without an immediate solution to a drastic problem with our main computer – and more so if the backup computer also has access to our cloud storage as describe in the previous point. A partial backup (synchronizing files that have been added or modified) also seems a reasonable option.

3. Make an archive of all our data, on a yearly basis. This backup would be used mainly for storage purposes, and would best be made to a distant physical location. An external hard drive –or two hard drives, used in rotation– would be perfect for this purpose. Stored in a friend's house, or in that of a family member, this hard drive would serve as a recovery scheme in the event of the really catastrophic loss of both our main computer, and of the backup machine. These backups should be complete copies of all our data. Set aside a period of the year when sufficient time is available to perform this task reliably and completely – and do so once a year!

Naturally, each person is the sole master of his or her backup scheme, and must decide what works best for their own workflow. The scheme set out in the tip above works well for the author. But it is proposed merely as an example, a base framework upon which each reader may elaborate as they see fit.

| **Tip:** One **never** has enough backups!

5.2 Why are we not speaking about RAID?

A backup can be seen as useful on one single condition: that it is actually made, and with a fairly high frequency. A backup that is not made in time, nor properly, will not give us a recovery strategy when –not if, but when– disaster strikes. It is for this reason that automating backups is always a good idea, since it takes part of the human factor out of it. With this view, techniques such as RAID (either hardware RAID or software) often come out when speaking about backups in a professional environment.

RAID is the acronym of *Redundant Array of Inexpensive Disks*. The basic idea behind this group of techniques is to replicate data across several physical disks. Data is written several times –sometimes twice, sometimes more or less often– on different physical supports, with the understanding that in the event that one of these physical disks fails, it will be possible to recover all data items from the other disks. Each time an element of data is written to disk, it must be written several times to ensure at least one of the copies will survive. On the other hand, each time an element of data is read back by the computer, it may be read from any one of these locations. Doing so in a parallel fashion gives us a nice boost in read speed, which is a secondary benefit of RAID techniques..

In actual practice in corporate environments, a further step has been to replace the 'I' in "Inexpensive" by the 'H' in "High-quality" or the 'E' in "Expensive", since using better and faster physical drives further reduces the possibility of losing a hard drive in the first place.

Naturally, GNU/Linux in general and Linux Mint in particular is very well placed to support both hardware RAID, when a specific piece of electronics take care of handling RAID operations, and software RAID, when it is the operating system that does so. Given this, the question remains why we do not advocate for individual users to use these techniques outside of a business environment.

The main argument is complexity. Handling more than one single physical disk creates complexity on several levels:

1. Just having several disk drives may be a hassle, or even impossible on mobile equipment such as a laptop. Modern, thin, form factors typically exclude inserting a second hard drive into the computer. Previously, a potential solution was to replace the optical –CD or DVD– drive with a carrier bay, allowing one to insert second SATA 2"1/2 form-factor hard drive in the place of this unit. However, modern equipment tends to eliminate the optical drives altogether.

2. RAID units must be monitored for failure. A tendancy has been observed for users to have complete confidence in their RAID setups, and omit to consult their state of health regularly. Unfortunately, it is not always evident when a RAID array has one disk gone bad. In such a case, it is urgent to replace the failing disk for a new one, and consolidate the complete array. Otherwise, a second hard drive failure is tantamount to losing data. This has happened quite often, with the aggravating factor that the hard drives in a RAID array tend to be of the same model and age; thus, when one disk fails, the others are likely also on the verge of doing so.

3. Using the software tools to rebuild a RAID array in which one disk has failed and been replaced may be seen as a rather technical endeavour, with which most "standard" users may not find within their comfort zones.

4. Using a RAID array gives absolutely no protection against the complete loss of a computer, be it by fire, theft or some other circumstance.

In final analysis, it is perhaps best not to rely on the potentially false sense of security that using a RAID array may give you, and instead concentrate on setting up and maintaining one or several proper backups.

5.3 Simple backups from the command line

5.3.1 Preparing our disks for backing up

Let us consider a simple setup for the purposes of example, where we wish to make a complete copy of all files in our user directory. We wish to make this copy to an external drive connected over USB. For our purposes, it is not relevant whether the external drive is a pen-drive, or an external hard drive. What counts is that is should have enough free space to hold a copy of our files.

Let us begin by opening a terminal window. The first command we should issue is `pwd`, to make sure we are inside our home directory. If we log in as user "user", then we should find ourselves inside folder /home/user:

```
$ pwd
/home/user
```

Now, the `du` command can be used to calculate the amount of space used. By default, it gives results for the folder *in which we are*, which explains my insistence on issuing `pwd` previously. Let us add option -s to sum up the sizes of all files in this folder (with any sub-folders), and option -h to specify a human-readable output format:

```
$ du -sh
24G    .
```

So, now we know the current folder –denoted '.'– contains a total of 24 GBytes of files. This is the amount of free space we will need to make a complete backup copy of our data.

> **Tip:** It is always best to allow ample space for backups. If we require 24 GBytes of space at the very least, allowing 25% more –or 30 MBytes– would be a reasonable minimum amount of free space to aim for.

Let us locate an external drive with enough free space on it, and connect it to our computer. Once this is done, begin by finding out which device letter the new device is using. We will use the same command, dmesg, as discussed in Chapter 2:

```
$ dmesg
  [... many lines ]
[17726.864040] scsi 6:0:0:0: Direct-Access       TOSHIBA
    MK2553GSX
[17726.864863] sd 6:0:0:0: Attached scsi generic sg2
    type 0
[17726.865381] sd 6:0:0:0: [sdb] 488397168 512-byte
    logical blocks: (250 GB/233 GiB)
[17726.866475] sd 6:0:0:0: [sdb] Write Protect is off
[17726.866486] sd 6:0:0:0: [sdb] Mode Sense: 28 00 00
    00
[17726.867549] sd 6:0:0:0: [sdb] No Caching mode page
    found
[17726.867554] sd 6:0:0:0: [sdb] Assuming drive cache:
    write through
[17727.215006]  sdb: sdb1
[17727.218903] sd 6:0:0:0: [sdb] Attached SCSI disk
```

```
[17727.898336] EXT4-fs (sdb1): mounted filesystem with
    ordered data mode. Opts: (null)
```

Here, we read that we have just connected a new drive, that is actually an external rotational hard disk, built by Toshiba and reporting model number MK2553GSX. This drive has been identified by the system as /dev/sdb1, and has a capacity of 250 GBytes[1].

Also, note that the first partition on this new drive, /dev/sdb1, has already been mounted on our computer. We can see more details using command df:

```
$ df -h
Filesystem       Size   Used    Free   %Us  Mounted on
    [...]
/dev/sda2         60G    38G     22G    65%  /
    [...]
/dev/sda1        197M   4,7M    193M     3%  /boot/efi
    [...]
/dev/sdb1         92G   462M     87G     1%  /media/user/USB
```

So, on my computer, the internal hard drive was /dev/sda, with two partitions mounted on /boot/efi and on / (the root of the file-system) respectively. We can also confirm the new external hard drive has a single partition, /dev/sdb1. Moreover, this partition does not occupy all the available space

---

[1]Hard drive capacities may be reported in Bytes, kBytes, MBytes, GBytes, etc, where each unit is precisely 1000 times the previous one. This unit is used by manufacturers. They may also be reported in "iBytes", kiB, MiB, GiB, etc, where each unit is 1024 times the previous one, or 2 to the power of 10. This is the older scheme, that most computer technicians still prefer. the "iB" units are larger than plain Bytes' units, so 250 GB = 250,000,000 Bytes = approximately 233 GiB = 233 times 1024 cubed. If this is not your terrain of choice, please do not worry – actual differences are quite small.

on the external drive, but a mere 92 GBytes (out of 250 GBytes). 87 GBytes are still available. This is ample for our needs, which stand at 24 GBytes[2].

Using command `mount`, we can see that the partition on the external drive has been mounted (i.e. made accessible) on `/media/user/USB`, and has file-system type 'ext4'. It has been mounted as *read-write* ('rw'), instead of *read-only* (which would be 'ro'):

```
$ mount | grep sdb
/dev/sdb1 on /media/user/USB type ext4
 (rw,nosuid,nodev,relatime,data=ordered,uhelper=
    udisks2)
```

Figure 5.1: The icon of an external hard drive, mounted automatically by the operating system.

When Linux Mint detects the presence of an external drive with partitions it can mount, it does so automatically. They appear as icons on the desktop, similar to Figure 5.1.

> If the system **cannot** mount the partitions on a newly-connected drive, they will still appear using the `dmesg` command. However, the system will not mount them, and a specific error message should appear in the output of `dmesg` giving us more information on which file-system the partitions are using.

---

[2]Observant readers will have noted that the space reported as used, 462 MBytes, plus that reported as free, 87 GBytes, does not add up to the total space on this partition. This is because GNU/Linux file-systems traditionally reserve 5% of the capacity of each partition for administrative uses.

We now need to have a word about file-system types. GNU/Linux can natively use different types of partition format, some of which are specific to this operating system, and some of which come from other operating systems:

- **ext4** or *Extended File System, version 4* is the main type used in GNU/Linux systems. It is considered very mature and sure to use, though it does lack some features found in more recent offerings. **btrfs** or *better FS* is one of these, though it has not –yet– gained the acceptance of ext4.

  Both of these file-system types will easy be mounted and read from on any GNU/Linux computer. However, little support is available from other operating systems, so use this option mainly for data that must be read and used only on GNU/Linux computers.

- **vfat** *Virtual FAT* was the main file-system used on Microsoft's Windows XP operating system. Readily read by many operating systems, it is often the file-system of choice for external devices and pen-drives. The newer **ntfs** *NT File System* dates back to Microsoft Windows NT. This more advanced system has some advantages over vfat, such as supporting *journaling*[3]. Linux Mint 19 comes with the `ntfs-3g` software package installed, which allows it to mount and read volumes formatted with the ntfs filesystem. This would perhaps be a good choice is using the external drive to share data with a Windows system.

- **hfs** *Hierarchical File System* and **apfs** *Apple File System* are two types of file-system used, basically, by Apple's Mac OS and very few other operating systems. Support for these in GNU/Linux is sketchy, as for many other operating systems.

---

[3]In essence, this means ntfs –like ext4 and many others– are less susceptible to damage if the computer suffers a power outage.

> **Tip:** If sharing information between computers with Apple Mac
> OS and GNU/Linux operating systems, copying files over the
> network –as discussed in the next section– is the way to go.

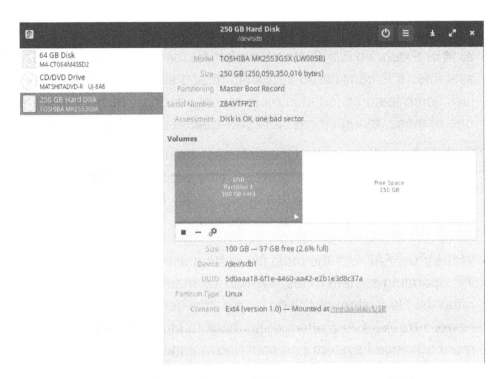

Figure 5.2: Using Gnome Disks on an external drive.

If the current partitioning scheme on the external drive is not satisfactory, it can be changed using the Gnome Disks application (Figure 5.2). This is usually installed by default on many Ubuntu derivatives and on Linux Mint, and accessible from the Menu, Accessories, Disks. Alternatively, it can be invoked from the terminal's command line using command `gnome-disks`.

Once running, be sure to **select the external drive**, not the internal hard disk, before performing any changes. Now, partitions can be deleted, created, edited, or formatted using a different file-system as desired. They will need to be unmounted before alterations are performed, using the square "stop" button. They can be re-mounted afterwards, using the triangular "play button.

5.3.2 Performing a complete or incremental backup

Finally, once the external drive has been formatted to our liking, we can proceed to make our backup.

Before starting to make the backup, let us begin by considering the information stored about each file. Regarding most file-systems, the system can report the name, size and modification date for each file[4]. The last bit, the date of last modification, will be crucial to any *incremental* backup scheme, since this is one of the techniques most backup tools use to determine whether a file has been modified or not since a previous backup was made.

For instance, consider the following sequence of commands:

```
$ ls -l easy_linux.tex
-rw-rw-r-- 1 user user 793 Aug.  4 14:25 easy_linux.
   tex
$ touch easy_linux.tex
$ ls -l easy_linux.tex
-rw-rw-r-- 1 user user 793 Aug.  4 16:25 easy_linux.
   tex
```

The ls command lists files in the current directory, following the UNIX style. The corresponding command for Microsoft Windows would be DIR.

---

[4]Some file-systems also store information on the date on which the file was originally created, as distinct from the last time of modification.

With the -l option, ls will give us a *long* printout for each file. In this case, it indicated the .tex file was last modified on August 4th, at 14:25. Next, the touch command was used to modify the file's date of modification. A subsequent use of ls will show us this file has been modified, at 16:25. When making an incremental backup of this file, the backup system should first examine the date stamped on the existing backup of this file, and if the date it reads is previous to August 4th at 16:25, it should make a new copy of the file inside the backup (overwriting the existing copy the backup currently holds).

A simple way of copying files to make a backup is, under GNU/Linux as under Mac OS or any UNIX variant, the cp "copy" command. However, unless care is taken –i.e., the '-a' option is not used– this command will overwrite the date of modification on the copy, setting it to the current time. Therefore, if we use this command to make a complete backup, that will later be updated with incremental backups, it is important to always put this option in. Another useful option is '-r', i.e. recursively copy, including the contents of folders and subsequent sub-folders.

Open a terminal window, and if our target drive is mounted on /media/user/USB, issue the command:

```
$ cp -ra * /media/user/USB/
```

If one starts receiving error messages concerning "Permission denied", this is because the directory on which the unit is mounted –i.e. /media/user/USB is not marked as being owned by the user, but by 'root', the administrator of the system. This can easily be worked around. Supposing, once more, that our login name is 'user', gain administrative permissions and change ownership of this folder:

```
$ sudo chown user.user /media/user/USB/
```

and then run the copy command once more. If opening the external drive from the desktop icon, one should be able to actually see the files and folders starting to appear as they are transferred over..

The only issue with the `cp` command is that is only useful for making complete backups. As the reader will have noted if a large number of files are involved, the backup process can be slowly, at times extremely so. For this reason, incremental backups are to be preferred. To perform one, the `rsync` command can be used. Simply mount the external drive as usual, open a terminal and:

```
$ rsync -aruv * /media/user/USB/
```

`rsync` is a very powerful utility that can copy files in between mounted disk drives, or even over the network. In this case, we are specifying options:

- `-a` to indicate archive mode.

- `-r` to recursively copy file from folders and sub-folders.

- `-u` to update and files that have been modified since the last backup was created.

- `-v` to be verbose about what is happening.

With this last option activated, `rsync` will output file names on screen in the terminal, as they are copied. This is very handy to keep track of what, precisely, is being done at any one time.

Another useful parameter with `rsync` is the `--exclude` command. This tells `rsync` not to make a backup of a specific file or folder (and its contents). This can be useful when part of our files are not wanted inside the backup. For instance, to exclude the Videos folder and its contents:

```
$ rsync -aruv * /media/user/USB/ --exclude=Videos
```

> **Tip:** This is why it may be useful to think about our backup strategy **before** starting to create content. Will we need to back up all our files? Or, will certain folders be backed up more often than others?
>
> According to our backup strategy, it may be interesting to place files that need to be backup up often, in a single folder, for instance in Documents. We then know that this folder is to be prioritized when backing up. On the other hand, rarely consulted and little modified documents may find a place in another folder, for instance Archives. This second folder will be backed up, but less often than Documents.

If we should ever need to **delete** a folder within a backup, we can use the `rm` command to do so recursively. For instance, to delete folder Videos and all its contents:

```
$ rm -r /media/user/USB/Videos
```

However, some care should be taken, since **rm will not ask permission** before performing any deletion. Deleted files fills also **will not be recoverable**. Specifically, ensure you are specifying the correct folder name (such as `/media/user/USB`). If no folder name is given, `rm` could very well erase files from the current directory, which could end up removing all files from your home directory.

Alternatively, erasing files using the file explorer application on the desktop is a safer option. In that situation, please do remember to empty the recycling bin, since files that have been transferred into there will still take up disk space.

5.4 Network backups and to the cloud

5.4.1 Backups over the local network

As stated previously, rsync is a very flexible and powerful program. It can synchronize files not only across locally-connected drives, but also between computers. To do so, it uses the Secure Shell (SSH) protocol.

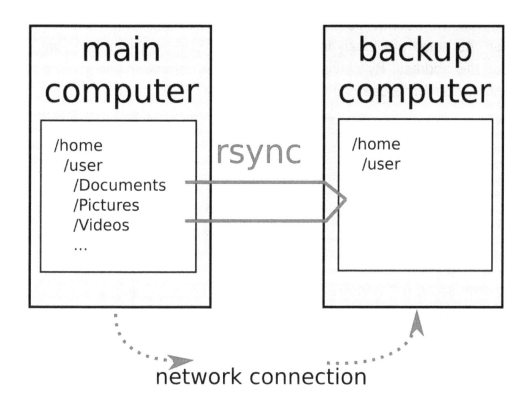

Figure 5.3: Using the rsync command to back up user data over a network.

Let us consider an example, in which two computers are connected to the same local network. The first (main) computer contains the originals of the user's files and folder, which now need to be backed up to the second computer (Figure 5.3).

Out first step will be to install an SSH server on the *second computer*. This will be acting as a server, receiving a connection from the first one. To so do, install the `openssh-server` package. The corresponding `openssh-client` package is installed by default on most GNU/Linux systems.

```
$ sudo apt install openssh-server
```

Now, we need to determine the IP address, also of the second computer. As noted previously in Chapter 3, the `ifconfig` command will give report this address. By *piping* the output of this command into `grep`, a command that performs searches, we can extract all IP addresses directly:

```
$ ifconfig | grep inet
        inet 127.0.0.1  netmask 255.0.0.0
        inet6 ::1  prefixlen 128  scopeid 0x10<host>
        inet 192.168.0.106  netmask 255.255.255.0
          broadcast 192.168.0.255
        inet6 fe80::cdeb:dbd6:6721:6da5  prefixlen 64
          scopeid 0x20<link>
```

The 127.0.0.1 address is the localhost address, and is not relevant. The address that will make this target computer visible on most networks is 192.168.0.106 . Naturally, the precise IP address returned will depend on the user's network setup.

Now, from the *main* computer, we can use `rsync` to make an incremental backup of all our user's files from the main computer to the backup machine:

This command may complain about not trusting the destination machine, specifically when the command is run for the first time. Simply reply 'yes' to make the destination machine trusted, and continue.

In the previous example, we suppose that the **same login name** is used on both computers. If this is not the case, use the following syntax, where `username` refers to the user's login name on the target computer:

```
$ rsync -aruv * username@192.168.0.106:/home/username/
```

> **Tip:** The rsync technique may also be used to back up files to a remote locality. However, to do so, the target's remote IP address must be visible from the main computer. This is generally difficult with the setup of most domestic networks; techniques such as *port forwarding* would need to be implemented on the target's router connecting it to the Internet.
>
> Needless to say, such a setup would best be left to professionals, or to network technicians with a full understanding of what they are doing. A badly constructed setup can leave one of the networks wide open to any threats coming in from the Internet – of which there are plenty.

5.4.2 Backing up to the cloud

With the ubiquity of cloud-based storage nowadays, using the cloud to back up files can seen an attractive proposition. The cloud provider will probably make more than one copy of user data in their own infrastructure, perhaps in different physical locations all around the world. This makes it difficult to actually loose data – unless, obviously, the cloud service provider goes out of business for whatever reason. Another concern would be data security, as in keeping our details safe from prying eyes.

For this reason, the procedure outlined in these lines will include the following steps:

1. Group all files (and sub-folders) that need to be backup up within a single folder, which we will simply call *Folder*. We will suppose this folder is in the user's home directory, i.e. /home/user.

2. Compress this folder. This will allow us to work on a single file, as opposed to a structure made up of many files and sub-folders. It will also remove much structure from the underlying data, making it more difficult for any potential hacker to gain insight into the structure of our data.

3. Encrypt the compressed folder.

4. Copy the compress and encrypted folder up into the cloud.

Step 1 would probably be best performed using graphical tools, such as the file explorer on the desktop. If files are already stored in an appropriate folder, this step can be omitted.

To compress the folder, we have several possibilities. Compressed file formats are legion in the UNIX and GNU/Linux worlds. However, the user will probably be more accustomed to the ZIP file format, and for this reason it is on this format we will work with. There are several ways of compressing a folder. From the terminal, we could issue the following command:

```
$ zip -r Folder.zip Folder
  adding: Folder/ (stored 0%)
  adding: Folder/jowens_kuai.jpg (deflated 2%)
  [...]
```

We should now see, in the file explorer, both the original folder and the compressed copy (Figure 5.4).

As an alternative, one can open the user's home directory from the desktop icon, and simply right-click on the Folder directory. There exists an

Figure 5.4: Compressing a folder into ZIP format.

Figure 5.5: Compressing a folder into ZIP format from the desktop.

option to compress the folder. Please do remember to select the appropriate compression type (Figure 5.5).

Let us proceed to step 3, and encrypt the ZIP file. There are several alternatives, mostly as regards the encryption algorithm to be used. For most cases, a simple symmetrical encryption such as the Advanced Encryption Standard (AES)[5] will be more than sufficient. Begin by selecting a *passphrase* that only you (or the person for whom the files are destined) will know. Be sure to select a passphrase that you will remember, since there is no practical way of recuperating data that has been encrypted using AES without this information.

Now, we will use the OpenSSL[6] software to encrypt the ZIP file:

---

[5]This algorithm is widely used in the encryption of mobile phones, and electronic commerce applications.

[6]Web page at: `https://www.openssl.org/`.

```
$ openssl enc -aes-265-cbc -in Folder.zip -base64 -out
    Folder.aes
enter aes-256-cbc encryption password:
Verifying - enter aes-256-cbc encryption password:
$ ls Folder* -lh
-rw-r--r-- 1 user user    21M Aug 5 12:12 Folder.aes
-rw-r--r-- 1 user user    16M Aug 5 11:58 Folder.zip
$ rm Folder.zip
```

With the openssl command, we have specified that we wish to encrypt -enc a file, that the input file is Folder.zip and the output to be created Folder.aes. The -base64 option is there to indicate the file is to be codified using the Base64 scheme, which turns its contents into a file that is readable by any text viewer – though with its contents in encrypted form. This helps ensure compatibility with cloud services, which may balk at files in pure binary form. Finally, housekeeping is done and the original ZIP file is deleted.

On to step 4, and the encrypted .aes file may be stored in the cloud, using the usual mechanisms provided by that service to upload a file.

> **Tip:** If storing the encrypted file in a cloud service that provides folder synchronization –such as Dropbox–, please make sure the compression and encryption are **not** performed within a folder that is being synchronized to the cloud. Otherwise, the cloud service provider would see (and presumably retain a copy) the files before encryption. In clear, do not do this inside the /home/user/Dropbox folder.
> Naturally, the same applies to any other cloud service provider and not only to the very satisfactory Dropbox service.

As for recovering data, the steps are much the same, but in reverse. Begin by downloading the encrypted file, into an appropriate location on your hard drive. Your home folder is probably a good place to start. Then, successively decrypt and unzip its contents. In a terminal:

```
$ openssl enc -d -aes-256-cbc  -in Folder.aes -base64
  -out Folder.zip
enter aes-256-cbc decryption password:
$ unzip Folder.zip
Archive:  Folder.zip
   creating: Folder/
  inflating: Folder/jowens_kauai.jpg
  [...]
$ rm Folder.zip Folder.aes
```

In the `openssl` command, please note the presence of the -d option, indicating decryption. Also note the -in and -out filename have been inverted. All other options still need to be present, if used during encryption. The `unzip` command requires no explanation. Finally, some more housekeeping is in order to remove excess files, and leave us only with the Folder folder.

5.5   Graphical tools

Recent versions of Linux Mint, and more specifically version 19, have been known to incorporate graphical backup applications of the Mint project's own design. Other distributions have also done the same. In this, GNU/Linux distributions are following the path traced by Apple OS and its famous (or infamous?) Time Machine[7].

---

[7]Time Machine has been criticized for lacking transparency as to precisely which operations are being carried out at any one time. In spite of this drawback, having automatic backups is generally recognized as a very useful feature and this application is in wide use.

In most cases, these are in essence graphical user interfaces that invoke the very same commands we have used from the terminal. However, they may come in handy, specially to automate the backup process.

Figure 5.6: The Timeshift system backup utility.

In Linux Mint 19, we can find the Timeshift system backup utility in Menu, Administration (Figure 5.6). Its purpose is basically to create (and maintain) a complete backup of our system. In the event that any changes we make to our system go wrong, the backup can then be used to retrieve and restore a previous state. From a backup standpoint, it would tend towards performing a system mirror, though the end result is a backup that **cannot** be used directly to boot our computer in the event of mishap, without further configuration[8].

---

[8]We shall not delve into making bootable backups. This is an advanced technique that should be attempted by users with some experience, well outside the scope of this book. We will give a pointer, however: a bootable backup will need to have a *bootloader* –such as GRUB– loaded onto the first sectors of the backup disk or partition.

> **Tip:** It is important to note for **which purposes** Timeshift has been designed. In its current form, it basically protects against **user error**, either by destroying data inadvertently or by altering the system configuration.
>
> It may be possible to restore a system involved in a hardware issue, from a Timeshift backup. The idea is that the system would be formatted and set up as new from the Linux Mint installation medium, and then the backup used in reverse to restore user data and software applications. This technique would certainly be interesting, but would need to be fully tested before relying on a Timeshift backup for this purpose.

> ▸ Snapshots are saved on the same disk from which they are created (system disk). Storage on other disks is not supported. If system disk fails then snapshots stored on it will be lost along with the system.

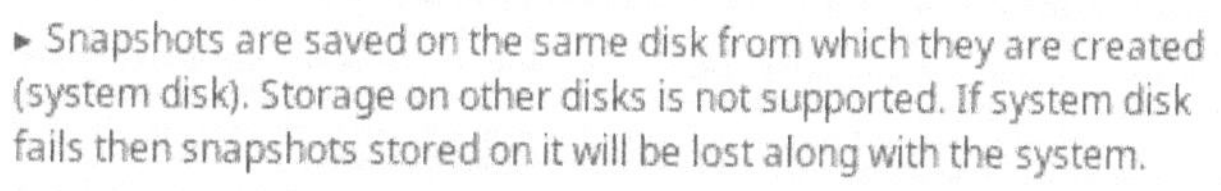

Figure 5.7: The BTRFS option for the Timeshift utility.

Timeshift proposes two techniques to create system backups. One, is based on the BTRFS file system. To use it, we would need to have our system installed on a partition formatted with this file-system, instead of the more ubiquitous *ext4* file-system proposed in the chapter on system installation. Since BTRFS is more recent than *ext4*, it contains extra features. One is the creation of *snapshots*, which are a way of creating a copy of the file-system. Between one snapshot and the next, the only data that will be stored are the differences that occur, and not the complete data set. As can be imagined, this technique can give us considerable savings in disk space. However, snapshots need to be created within the very same volume as the original file-system (Figure 5.7). For this reason, if our hard drive were to fail, having a BTRFS backup would not preserve us against data loss: both out main copy and any snapshots would all be inaccessible from their position the failed drive.

> **Tip:** In our modern world, where laptops and mobile computing use is widespread, hard drive –specially the rotation type– are exposed to physical shocks and potentially harmful variations in their electrical supplies. Together with screens and keyboards, laptops' hard drives are known to be one of the components of such computer with the highest failure rates.

> **Tip:** One can observe that Timeshift is based upon existing tools, the *rsync* command, and the BTRFS file system. These could be applied by hand, through the terminal, as discussed previously concerning *rsync*.

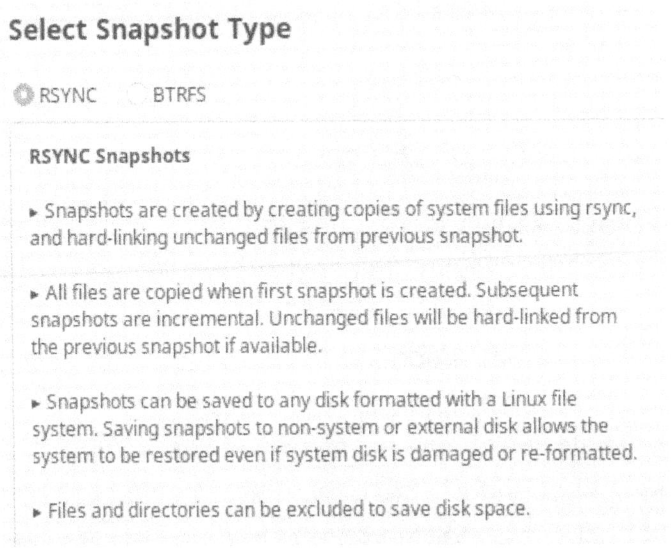

Select Snapshot Type

○ RSYNC   ○ BTRFS

RSYNC Snapshots

▸ Snapshots are created by creating copies of system files using rsync, and hard-linking unchanged files from previous snapshot.

▸ All files are copied when first snapshot is created. Subsequent snapshots are incremental. Unchanged files will be hard-linked from the previous snapshot if available.

▸ Snapshots can be saved to any disk formatted with a Linux file system. Saving snapshots to non-system or external disk allows the system to be restored even if system disk is damaged or re-formatted.

▸ Files and directories can be excluded to save disk space.

Figure 5.8: The rsync option for the Timeshift utility.

The alternative technique for making backups in Timeshift is through the use of the *rsync* command. This is, in our view, much to be preferred for its flexibility for general use. Backups are independent of their original file-system, so can be placed on an external drive (Figure 5.8).

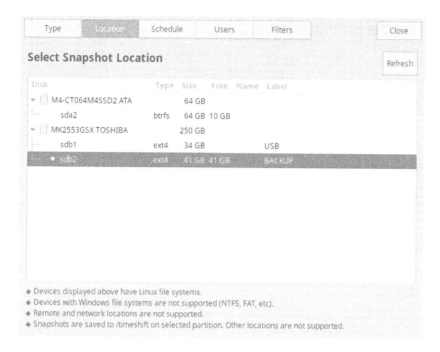

Figure 5.9: Choosing in which unit to place rsync backups.

As we continue through the initial setup wizard, Timeshift will need to know in which unit (drive and partition) to place backups (Figure 5.9). In this case, an external unit with two partitions has been connected to the computer, and the second partition (/dev/sdb2) specified as the location for backups. However, perhaps this would be a good moment to reflect on this choice. The Timeshift utility will typically be used to automate making backups. So, logically, the user will have a natural tendency to program this activity for times in which the computer will likely be running, but nobody is actually working at the keyboard. In such times, will the external drive be connected and available to Timeshift?

If the reply is "maybe not", perhaps we would either need to choose another disk drive, preferably one that will in all likelihood be permanently connected to the computer at that time, or choose another time to program backups.

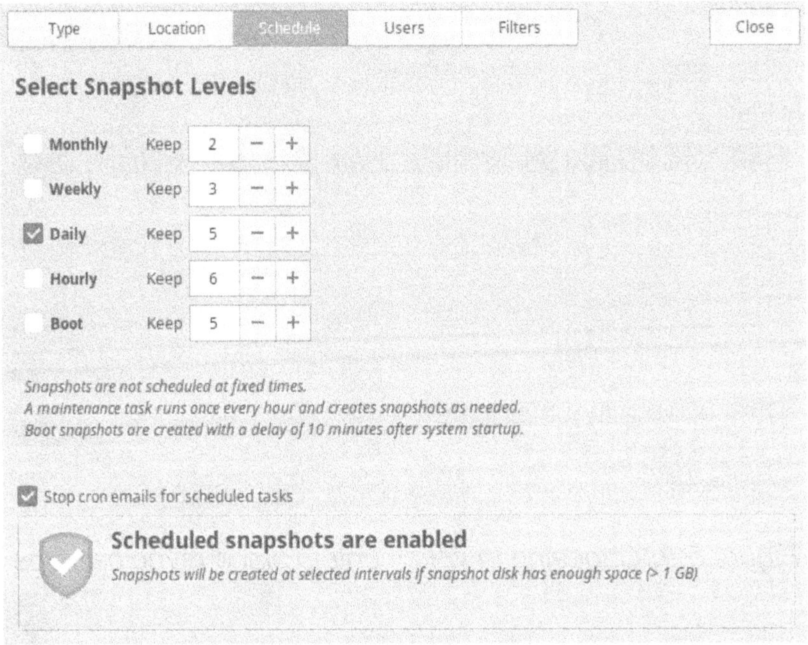

Figure 5.10: Programming the time when to perform backups.

In the next screen (Figure 5.10), the user can choose when to perform backups. The actual choice –monthly, weekly, daily or more often– depends on the user. However, in practice the default choice of "daily" can perhaps be seen as reasonable for environments in which many changes are made to files each day, such as with a business or professional use of the computer. For many domestic situations, the "weekly" choice could perhaps be seen as sufficient.

In any case, the number of snapshot levels can be fine-tuned, in order to specify how many backups may be present on the support at any one time. When the number of backups exceeds the level given, older backups are deleted. This mechanism can be useful to avoid overfilling the backup location.

Figure 5.11: Should user directories be backed up?

As seen in Figure 5.11, the next step in configuring Timeshift involves choosing whether to back up, or not, users' home folders. This option can be given on a per-user basis, with the system administrator *root* as a supplementary option.

He, too, the choice belongs to the user. In a domestic environment, your choice should probably be a resounding YES!, if you are using Timeshift at all to perform backups. In a professional use-case, however, things may become a tad more complicated. Depending on company policy guidelines, documents may need to be backed up to a central server[9].

If in doubt, it is probably best to include user documents in backups – and to make sure, by actually going through the backup files, that their documents are actually being backup up correctly.

> **Tip:** The next configuration panel, Filters, allows the user to specify specific inclusions or exclusions in the backup scheme. This is a very practical feature when large items –such as video files– are not to be included in the backup so as not to take up much space.

---

[9]On this server, backups will most probably be performed on a regular basis by technicians.

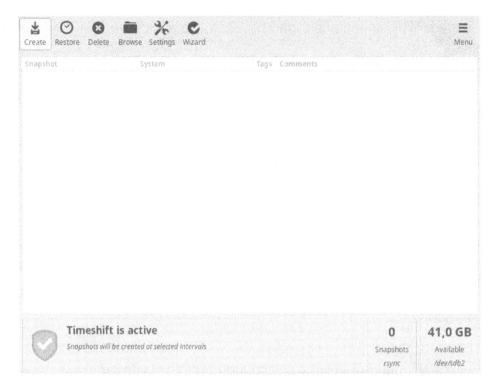

Figure 5.12: The Timeshift utility main panel.

Once the wizard has been completed, the Timeshift main screen appears (Figure 5.12). It will be presented directly to the user the next time the application is run.

At this point, automatic backups have already been programmed. If the user should wish to alter their configuration, the Settings button will give access to the same configuration screen used in the wizard. The other buttons are available, to create manually a new backup, restore the system from a backup, delete a backup, and browse existing backups. Finally, one can run the initial wizard once more.

> **Tip:** Perhaps the most interesting bit of information in Timeshift's main screen is located in the bottom lower corner: it is the amount of free space left in the support for making backups.
>
> This amount needs to be closely monitored, and the support changed for a larger one if free space shows any sign of going below what is currently used up on the computer's main hard drive.
>
> The morale is that **backup drives need to be larger** than the computer's main drive. Luckily, disk space is rather economical these days.

5.6   Some final thoughts

In this chapter, we reviewed the various backup strategies available for GNU/Linux systems. Several tools are available to perform backups, whether they be a very simple copy to a locally connected external drive, or a backup strategy that makes use of our local network or of a cloud service.

A backup strategy can only protect our data against specific dangers. For this reason, it must be designed taking into account our precise needs and potential causes for data loss. Saving our data from an incident with hardware will lead us to use various physical supports. Preparing for possible user error would imply having more than one copy of the information, though it may not be imperative to use different supports. In general terms, however, the more copies we have and the farther away –in geographical terms– they are from our main computer, the more chances we put on our side not to lose any data.

A failing computer may be fixed, at worst, by buying a new one. A failing operating system can easily be remedied by reinstalling a fresh copy from the ISO file. But lost data could very well not be recoverable at all, or end up being very costly to so do if at all possible. At the price, an external drive or a separate computer to store backup copies may appear as a rather economical solution – if used properly (i.e. frequently).

Chapter 6

Firewalls, malware and system protection

One of the reasons many users have to take an interest in GNU/Linux is the sense that this operating system may give greater security that other offerings. In recent years, however, a series of incidents have shown that, along with the increase in usage numbers for GNU/Linux in general, so have the number of computer viruses and malware in the general sense gone up. Since many servers on the Internet now run some form of Linux[1], it follows that those who make malware should be more interested in this technology.

General-purpose users of a GNU/Linux laptop or desktop may be asking themselves how this phenomenon could impact them, and whether they should be at all apprehensive about such matters.

---

[1]Commercial operating systems for servers tend to be rather costly. Since licensing is often quoted in terms of numbers of servers or numbers of users, it makes economic sense for integrators of cloud-based services to prefer open-source operating systems, perhaps spending some money on a paid service contract with distributions that offer such services to businesses. Examples include RedHat and SuSE Linux, among others.

6.1   General considerations

Let us begin by proposing a qualified answer to the question above: we –all users of computing devices– should be apprehensive of malware and other attacks over the Internet. No computer or operating system can be certified to be completely free of security defects or other ways the "bad guys" could get in. Given time, they may very well get to it.

That being said, there are two factors that advocate in favor of GNU/Linux systems, versus other offerings:

- One is that the underlying operating system is based on a UNIX design, and open-source. The first factor tells us that the basic underlying framework is sound, and has been extensively developed from day one as a multitasking, multi-user environment. With this focus, it comes naturally that each user must be protected in some form from the actions of other users. This standpoint can easily be extended to a computer that is connected to the Internet, where the term "other users" may not be limited to users physically present at this computer.

  The fact that GNU/Linux has been developed from its beginnings with an open-source philosophy is also relevant. This means each piece of code that goes into the system is open for public scrutiny. Whenever an issue develops, it does so in a very public manner, and so can be identified and remedied – fast This is not always the case in a closed-source environment, where simply not that people obtain access to the source code and can scrutinize it for correctness.

- A second factor is that GNU/Linux systems have seen a sharp increase in their usage in servers. However, this increase has not yet been quite as visible in desktop and laptop usage. For this reason, desktop systems have not, as yet, been quite as often a target for the makers of malware.

To put the above into perspective, the reader could observe that both domestic routers, and mobile devices with the Android operating system are among the classes of electronic (computing) devices that have the worst reputation among those with a GNU/Linux operating system. These are also the very same classes of device that:

a) Are not very often updated, if ever.

b) Have been sold in the largest quantities, in any case much more than laptop or desktop computers running GNU/Linux.

> **Tip:** Always keep your computers and other devices up-to-date! When considering buying a new device, consider whether the manufacturer guarantees the availability of support, and for what period. In the absence of this information, take note of this manufacturer's track record in this sense. For devices that are locked in to a specific manufacturer and/or operating system, the availability of updates may very well be a limiting factor for the reasonable lifespan of the device.

As a final thought, readers should note that **no operating system is foolproof**. Although more secure than others, the increasing use of GNU/Linux operating systems is making them a more interesting target for potential attackers than in previous times. Some security precautions do need to be taken, thus minimizing the risks that, unfortunately, remain very much a fact of our times.

In the following sections, we will review the three main routes via which malware and various attacks can get into our system.

6.2   Installing software

The first route used by many viruses and other malware is by simply bundling itself with another –trustworthy– application. When the user installs the second application, the process unfortunately also installs a concealed payload. This would be the "Trojan Horse" approach.

The reader may have noted that, in the previous chapters, most software has been found in well-known locations. Be they the distribution's repositories, or well-known web pages, these sources of software are known to be safe. Very few cases have been noticed of malware getting into GNU/Linux repositories, a fact that can be directly attributed to the open-source nature of the software that goes in[2].

There are other means of obtaining software for GNU/Linux systems. One way is by adding a project repository to our system, in addition to the distribution's. These are situations in which the project managers ask you to use the `apt-add-repository` command, such as is almost always the case with the Ubuntu's Launchpad[3]. As with a direct download of an executable program, **some caution** must be applied. A very high percentage of such projects are totally *bona fide*. However, downloading software to run on the user's computer must be seen as somewhat an act of trust: do we really trust these people, or should we pass on their application and search for a better-known alternative, even if it does not offer all the latest bells and whistles?

---

[2]The same can be said of software that is distributed in the form of source code since, by its nature, its contents and features are immediately visible to the end-user.

[3]Launchpad, at `https://launchpad.net/`.

> **Tip:** A quick browse through a project's forum pages and other online resources will often be sufficient to establish that their software offering is probably to be trusted. Some positive signs to look for are projects that are "mature", i.e. have been well-established for a period of time, have a user-base, and show some activity in the last period.
>
> If in doubt, adopt a position of caution and stick to the repositories of your distribution. You have already trusted them with the operating system on your computer, so you might as well continue trusting them as regards the rest of the software.

6.3   Controlling network services

A second route through which unauthorized access may be achieved in computers in by accessing the device over the network. This would be the main option for an attacker wishing to compromise a server; most servers are physically located in secure environments to which it is very difficult for unauthorized people to gain access. Think security guards and electronic key cards to open doors – literally.

The user of a normal desktop or laptop may not perceive living with the same degree of risk as for a server. However, this perception is at times false. In previous times, expensive connection charges made many users connect to the Internet only when service was actually needed. Their computers remained disconnected for a large proportion of the day, during which they were obviously not accessible for attackers. Nowadays, flat rates and ubiquitous connections have made the situation change, and most user's laptops and desktops stay connected to the Internet from 12 to 24 hours a day, thus increasing their exposure to attacks.

A second point worth bearing in mind is that, specifically with laptops and mobile computers, the user may connect at various times using wireless technology through access points and infrastructure that is not in their direct control. Coffee shops and various public networks that offer service over WiFi are typical situations in which one cannot make any assumptions about other users, or about the standard of the network material (routers and access points) used in setting up that network. The level of trust we can accord to such public networks must be, correspondingly, rather low.

To protect ourselves against the types of danger found in such environments, the user needs to put three basic mechanisms in place:

1. Be aware of their own browsing habits, and of the possibilities of downloading malware themselves.

2. Shut down any unnecessary services on their computer.

3. Install and use a firewall, if necessary.

The first point is often a question of common sense. Various online services are often known for containing questionable content; such places are also likely to contain malware to spring upon the unwary. Unfortunately, bona fide server have also been known to have been compromised, and used as a vector to infect unwary users. For this reason, computer owners are increasingly dependent on the quality of their web browsers, the piece of software that is in the first line to guard against malicious downloads.

For this reason, using major-brand web browsers, and **keeping them up-to-date** is a major step in avoiding malware downloads. As seen in the chapter on maintaining our system:

```
$ sudo bash
```

```
# apt update
# apt upgrade firefox
```

  or

```
$ sudo bash
# apt update
# apt upgrade google-chrome-stable
```

should have your back covered.

> **Tip:** With GNU/Linux as with any other operating system, if any part of the software requires a strict policy of keeping up to date, it is the web browser.
>
> Also: please **read and understand** any warnings displayed by the browser. Majors browsers such as Mozilla Firefox and Google's Chrome can often warn us of potential dangers. Make good use of this feature.

The second point that users can work on to protect themselves is to reduce exposure from attacks on services we may have running. A modern computer often runs various services, in order to allow the user to connect and share files from one computer to another, or to connect to a printer, or for other reasons. To give an example of what a reasonably well-configured computer shares, let us ask the system which *demons* (individual services) are running:

```
$ netstat -l
Active Internet connections (only servers)
Proto Recv-Q Send-Q Local Address          Foreign
   Address
tcp        0      0 localhost:17603        0.0.0.0:*
```

```
tcp      0        0 0.0.0.0:netbios-ssn      0.0.0.0:*
tcp      0        0 localhost:domain         0.0.0.0:*
tcp      0        0 0.0.0.0:ssh              0.0.0.0:*
tcp      0        0 localhost:ipp            0.0.0.0:*
tcp      0        0 0.0.0.0:microsoft-ds     0.0.0.0:*
tcp      0        0 localhost:17600          0.0.0.0:*
tcp6     0        0 [::]:netbios-ssn         [::]:*
tcp6     0        0 [::]:ssh                 [::]:*
tcp6     0        0 ip6-localhost:ipp        [::]:*
tcp6     0        0 [::]:microsoft-ds        [::]:*
udp  26112        0 localhost:domain         0.0.0.0:*
udp   8064        0 0.0.0.0:bootpc           0.0.0.0:*
udp  48768        0 0.0.0.0:netbios-ns       0.0.0.0:*
udp  50176        0 0.0.0.0:netbios-dgm      0.0.0.0:*
udp      0        0 0.0.0.0:51388            0.0.0.0:*
udp      0        0 0.0.0.0:ipp              0.0.0.0:*
udp  40960        0 0.0.0.0:17500            0.0.0.0:*
udp  11648        0 0.0.0.0:mdns             0.0.0.0:*
udp6     0        0 [::]:44055               [::]:*
udp6 48640        0 [::]:mdns                [::]:*
raw6     0        0 [::]:ipv6-icmp           [::]:* 7
```

It may come as a surprise that a personal computer should offer just so many services over the network. Let us break this list down to manageable chunks of information. In the first, place, one needs to know that, today, most local network services are offered using the very same core technology that makes the Internet work. This is known under the acronym TCP/IP. There are, currently, two main families of TCP/IP protocols used: those based on the fourth version of the protocol stack, noted IPv4, and those based on the newer IPv6.

Most computing networks –and access to the Internet in general– currently use IPv4. There has been much talk about adopting IPv6, mostly to counter the lack of IP addresses for servers under the IPv4 scheme. However, the transition, while underway, is going rather more slowly that expected. While it takes place, most operating systems offer both schemes at once, thus catering to users using the more traditional IPv4, or to others whose Internet Service Providers (ISPs) have been more proactive and have transitioned to IPv6.

The two protocol stacks are largely independent. For this reason, a computer that wishes to offer a service will, largely, need to offer it twice: once using the IPv4 stack, and once using IPv6.

In addition, services can be offered using either the connection-based protocol TCP, or the connection-less UDP. This is why we see four different categories of connection in the list of services:

- `tcp` for TCP over IPv4,

- `tcp6` for TCP over IPv6,

- `udp` for UDP over IPv4, and

- `udp6` for UDP over IPv6.

In addition, we also a raw service offered over IPv6, which corresponds to ECHO service on this service stack.

Since most services will be offered in the same way over both protocols, we can concentrate on IPv4 for the purposes of this discussion. Let us filter out IPv6:

```
Proto  Recv-Q Send-Q Local Address            Foreign
    Address
```

tcp	0	0	localhost:17603	0.0.0.0:*
tcp	0	0	0.0.0.0:netbios-ssn	0.0.0.0:*
tcp	0	0	localhost:domain	0.0.0.0:*
tcp	0	0	0.0.0.0:ssh	0.0.0.0:*
tcp	0	0	localhost:ipp	0.0.0.0:*
tcp	0	0	0.0.0.0:microsoft-ds	0.0.0.0:*
tcp	0	0	localhost:17600	0.0.0.0:*
udp	26112	0	localhost:domain	0.0.0.0:*
udp	8064	0	0.0.0.0:bootpc	0.0.0.0:*
udp	48768	0	0.0.0.0:netbios-ns	0.0.0.0:*
udp	50176	0	0.0.0.0:netbios-dgm	0.0.0.0:*
udp	0	0	0.0.0.0:51388	0.0.0.0:*
udp	0	0	0.0.0.0:ipp	0.0.0.0:*
udp	40960	0	0.0.0.0:17500	0.0.0.0:*
udp	11648	0	0.0.0.0:mdns	0.0.0.0:*

The first thing to note is that any services with the local address localhost are being offered only to this computer. Any attempts to connect from other computers on the network will not be accepted by the demon process. Thus, the localhost:domain service is a Domain Name Resolution (DNS) service[4], that is only available to programs –such as the web browser– running on our machine. Printers are also made available to all programs over the service labelled localhost:ipp, using the Internet Printing Protocol (ipp).

> **Tip:** In general terms, users should not need to worry about services offered only to localhost.

---

[4]DNS is a service that translates from a URL-type of address, to the actual IP address a client would need to connect to in order to obtain this service. Thus, a user could give a URL such as https://www.google.com, while the browser would in fact connect to an IP address such as 172.217.168.164 sing IPv4, or 2a00:1450:4003:80a::2004 using IPv6.

Services offered to 0.0.0.0 are available to any computer, connecting on any network interface, and thus will be accessible to other computers. In some cases, a single service may need to offer several components, on different ports. This is what has happened in the above example, where Windows file sharing had been enabled. This involves demons on: *0.0.0.0:netbios-ssn* and *0.0.0.0:microsoft-ds* over TCP, and *0.0.0.0:netbios-ns* and *0.0.0.0:netbios-dgm* over UDP. On a GNU/Linux system, these services are offered using the Samba server, an open-source implementation of Windows file sharing protocols[5].

Windows file sharing is a service that allows computers running different operating systems –there are clients for GNU/Linux and Apple Mac OS, as well as Microsoft's offerings– to share files, printers and other information over a local network. The system is based on each computer's announcing periodically its presence on the network. This leads to increased network activity, but can also become a security defect when the computer is used in an unprotected network situation since it can leak quite a lot of information about the operating system and its users. For this reason, we need to have a think if, indeed, we need to have the Samba server running on our computer, or if it is best not. On this particular computer, Samba had been installed using:

```
$ sudo bash
# apt install samba samba-client
```

and then configured by editing file /etc/samba/smb.conf, and adding users to Samba with command smbpasswd -a <username>.

If so desired, Samba can be completely removed from a computer using command:

---

[5]Fun fact: Samba is also used on Apple's Mac OS to connect to Windows machines and share files and printers.

```
$ sudo bash
# apt purge samba samba-client
```

Finally, Samba services may be temporarily halted, and started once more. This may be useful on a laptop that is mostly used within a controlled environment –such as a home or business network–, but may at times need to connect to the Internet over a less secure network. In such cases, **before** connecting to the network, one can issue the following command to halt Samba services:

```
$ sudo bash
# systemctl stop smbd.service
# systemctl stop nmbd.service
```

Please note there are two demons involved. Obviously, the corresponding commands could be used to re-start these services, using "start" instead of "stop". Services can also be marked to be started at boot time, using "enable". Alternatively, on a computer that will sometimes need Samba services but where one does not wish such services start at boot time, one could use "disable":

```
$ sudo bash
# systemctl disable smbd.service
# systemctl disable nmbd.service
```

> **Tip:** To determine whether a service is enabled or disabled, or if it is currently running, use command `systemctl status smbd.service` for a specific service, or `systemctl status` (without specifying a specific service) to get information on all services installed on the computer.

Once Samba is either removed, or disabled, the number of active services are now rather diminished. Visible from the network are now only:

- SSH, which is used to `rsync` files to this computer.

- Dropbox's local network synchronization protocol, `db-lsp`.

- BootP, which is part of if the mechanism to get an IP address automatically.

- IPP, listening for any other printers being shared on the local network over the Internet Printing Protocol.

- Multicast Domain Name Server (MDNS), used to convert local network computer names into IP addresses.

```
Proto  Recv-Q  Send-Q  Local  Address          Foreign
       Address
tcp         0       0  0.0.0.0:ssh            0.0.0.0:*
tcp         0       0  0.0.0.0:db-lsp         0.0.0.0:*
udp     10752       0  0.0.0.0:bootpc         0.0.0.0:*
udp         0       0  0.0.0.0:53470          0.0.0.0:*
udp         0       0  0.0.0.0:ipp            0.0.0.0:*
udp     37120       0  0.0.0.0:17500          0.0.0.0:*
udp    213504       0  0.0.0.0:17500          0.0.0.0:*
udp     26880       0  0.0.0.0:mdns           0.0.0.0:*
```

In addition, there are two other ports on which services are available: port number 53470 and port 17500. Investigating further in file /etc/services, a definition exists which points us to 17500 being assigned to the Dropbox local network synchronization protocol db-lsp (on UDP, as well as TCP). As for port 53470, the lsof (List Open Files) command tells us it is being used by the Avahi Daemon, which is also part of mDNS. This last command needs to be run with administrative privileges, since we are examining system processes.

```
$ cat /etc/services | grep 17500
db-lsp 17500/tcp    # Dropbox LanSync Protocol
$ sudo bash
# lsof | grep :53470
avahi-dae 940 avahi 14u IPv4 23142 0t0 UDP *:53470
```

> **Tip:** The author is aware that this section may have entered into rather more technical details than most readers will require. The point is that all these services –and many others– are regularly run by all modern operating systems. However, gaining a clear idea of what, precisely, is going on behind the scenes can be a tad complicated, and involve running specialized software. Under GNU/Linux, with a simple terminal and a reasonable grasp of the underlying concepts, all the information can slowly and surely be ferreted out, even by people who are not computer scientists.
>
> This fact should give us some confidence in the inner working of the operating system. It may also be of help if requiring technical assistance in case of mishap, since we have access to the information needed to help the technician establish a diagnostic, and to confirm that the diagnostic does, in fact, fit in with the facts. Having access to more information is never a bad thing.

6.4   Using a firewall

A *firewall* is, in essence, a piece of software that stands between the computer's operating system and the network. It filters connections in both directions. Some functions include:

- Allowing access from the network only to selected services.

- Allowing access from the network, only to specific computers or networks (determined by their IP addresses).

- Allowing access from the computer **outbound** to the network only to selected services or computers, i.e. filtering *outbound* communications.

- Monitoring and registering communications patterns and apply restrictions on traffic volumes.

The first two features are routinely implemented by all firewalls. The third is less used, although useful to restrict the possibilities any malware that has for some reason been installed on a computer to "call home" and contact its control server. A further application of restricting outbound connections would be as an ad blocker: working at the level of the operating system, a block set in place within the firewall can make connections to one or several servers impossible from all web browsers at once. The same could be said concerning implementing a control over access to certain services, as a form or parental control.

Finally, the fourth feature is used mainly on servers that are connected to the Internet, both as a means of controlling internal activity but also as a form of intrusion detection. It is, indeed, possible to implement it even on a laptop or small desktop computer running GNU/Linux. However, the details of such an application are quite technical and outside the scope of this book.

Setting up a firewall within Linux Mint is rather easy, since the Linux kernel has built-in firewall capacities. In addition, the Uncomplicated Firewall (ufw) software package is installed by default. The firewall can be turned on and off, and configured by hand using the ufw command. However, graphical tools are readily available. Begin by navigating to the Control Center in the Menu preferences (Figure 6.1).

Figure 6.1: The icon of the Control Center in the desktop menu's preferences.

Figure 6.2: The icon of the Firewall application within the Control Center.

Now scroll down within the Control Center, to the Firewall icon within the Administration section (Figure 6.2).

A very basic rule set can now easily be put in place (Figure 6.3). In essence, we permit all outgoing connections, so we can browse the Web or do whatever else we need to do, such as upgrading system software, connecting to a network printer, etc. We are blocking all inbound connections, so others cannot connect to any services offered by our computer. The **master switch** for the firewall has been turned on, thus enabling filtering.

This basic scheme will probably suit the needs of most users. However, it can be fine-tuned using the following Rules tab, in order to make specific services available to others.

Figure 6.3: Configuring the Firewall with a basic rule set.

Tip: When in doubt, refuse external access to a service. Most firewall schemes follow the basic principle of refusing all connections, and then specifically opening access to certain services.

Tip: A common error when using firewalls is to set up a rule granting external access to a service, for a specific task – and then forgetting about it. The hole in our computer's security stays open, until we close it back up.

If using a firewall and making changes from time to time, please make a point of reviewing the rules being implemented on a regular schedule.

Chapter 7

Concluding remarks

In the introduction, we set out our goals of providing some guidance for people who wish to delve into the world of GNU/Linux. What we may have achieved, or so we hope, is to show that this computing environment that at times may com across as a tad wild and weird –mostly to people with some technical background in other systems– is, in fact, rather tame. It is populated by the so-called "normal" people, who have a real job to do and need simple, dependable tools to do it.

In Chapter 2, we described how to install a base Linux Mint 19 operating system. Along we way, we chose to give the reader some vocabulary, concerning just what a GNU/Linux distribution is or what a Live Image may be useful for. We have tried to keep the technical jargon to a minimum. However, some technical aspects to need to be described, as when setting up any complex structure or process.

In Chapters 3 and 4, we wrote about maintaining the selection of software that comes, as standard, in the Linux Mint distribution, and about have to install supplementary software packages. This aspect is perhaps that which will feel slightly strange to users of other operating systems, due to the broad use of software repositories in the Linux Mint and Ubuntu worlds. This is a feature not restricted to these GNU/Linux distributions, but can be found in one form or another in mainstream distributions such as Debian –from which the `apt` package management system has been inherited, so to speak–, the RedHat / Fedora Linux / CentOS spread of distributions, and OpenSuSE. In all cases, using repositories and a tool such as `apt` is arguably more convenient and just plain *faster* than needing to download various pieces of software from different web pages, and perhaps in varying formats. However, since open- and free software is much about freedom, developers are free to provide software in other formats, such as snaps, flatpak, and AppImage. Users are also free –and, indeed, encouraged– to try these out, and to determine which option is most convenient for their own purposes.

Chapter 5 concerned making backups of user data, or even of the entire operating system, while Chapter 6 gave an alternatively quick summary of how to protect our system from malware and intrusions over the network. Both of these subjects deserve complete treatises on the matter and, indeed, such have been written and are widely available in any good collection of technical literature on computer server management. In this book, we needed to restrict ourselves to a level of detail that the aforesaid "normal" user can use to quickly set up a working system, and be somewhat confident of not begin in too much danger of losing data, nor too obvious a target for possible malicious activity on the Internet. If the reader is at all interested in such matters, we encourage him or her to read further and gain more technical knowledge and skills.

The beauty of an open GNU/Linux platform is that it can cater as well to those who simply need a dependable tool to suit their own everyday computing needs, and also to others who can use it as a tool to further study computer engineering and the field of information sciences in general.

In any case, this book has been written on a platform that has served the author well, and for many years. I only hope the same is true of our readers. For this reason, I would like to conclude by wishing you all happy –and trouble-free– computing!

www.ingramcontent.com/pod-product-compliance
Lightning Source LLC
Chambersburg PA
CBHW060147060326
40690CB00018B/4015